Discovering Welsh History · Book 4

Wales, Yesterday and Today

Geraint H. Jenkins

Oxford University Press 1990

The publishers wish to thank the following
for their permission to reproduce copyright material:

p. 6 National Museum of Wales (WFM); p. 7 National Museum of Wales (WFM); p. 8
National Library of Wales; p. 9 National Library of Wales; p. 11 National Museum of Wales
(WFM); p. 12 top Jeffrey F. Morgan, centre National Museum of Wales (WFM), bottom left
Institute of Agricultural History and Museum of English Rural Life, University of Reading,
bottom right Jeffrey F. Morgan; p. 13 top left, centre and bottom Massey Ferguson UK Ltd., top
right Alfa Laval, Cwmbrân; p. 14 National Museum of Wales (WFM); p. 15 National
Museum of Wales (WFM); p. 16 RLM Photographic; p. 17 top left and bottom RLM
Photographic, top right National Museum of Wales (WFM); p. 18 Harold Richards
Photography; p. 19 National Library of Wales; p. 20 Clwyd Record Office; p. 21 Welsh
History Resources Unit (WJEC); p. 23 top left Topham Picture Library, bottom right Central
Electricity Generating Board; p. 25 bottom left National Library of Wales, bottom right
Macdonald/Aldus Archive; p. 27 National Library of Wales; p. 29 left Clwyd Record Office,
right National Library of Wales; p. 30 National Library of Wales; p. 31 Tegwyn Roberts;
p. 33 top right John Brennan, centre left National Library of Wales, bottom right University
College of Wales, Aberystwyth; p. 34 National Museum of Wales (WFM); p. 35 top right
National Library of Wales, bottom left Jeffrey F. Morgan, with the kind permission of the
family; p. 36 Jeffrey F. Morgan; p. 37 top Jeffrey F. Morgan, bottom, with the kind permission
of the family of the late Sir Ifan ab Owen Edwards; p. 39 left BBC Cymru, right National
Library of Wales; p. 40 top Lyndon Jones, bottom Cymdeithas yr Iaith Gymraeg; p. 41 left
Jeffrey F. Morgan, right The Cartoon Film Company; p. 42 Welsh Industrial and Maritime
Museum; p. 43 John Brennan; p. 44 Wales Tourist Board; p. 45 Welsh Industrial and
Maritime Museum; p. 46 left Cyril Batstone, right John Brennan; pp. 47 and 48 Welsh
Industrial and Maritime Museum; p. 49 background National Library of Wales, centre Welsh
Industrial and Maritime Museum; pp. 50 and 53 Welsh Industrial and Maritime Museum;
p. 54 left Welsh Industrial and Maritime Museum, right Ffilmiau'r Nant; pp. 55, 57 and 59
Welsh Industrial and Maritime Museum; p. 60 top National Library of Wales/Western Mail
& Echo Ltd., bottom Welsh Industrial and Maritime Museum; p. 61 Welsh Industrial and
Maritime Museum; p. 62 South Wales Miners' Library; pp. 63 and 64 National Library of
Wales; p. 65 left Western Mail & Echo Ltd., right Imogen Young; p. 66 National Library of
Wales; p. 67 Imperial War Museum; p. 68 left National Museum of Wales (WFM), right
Jeffrey F. Morgan; p. 69 Welsh Industrial and Maritime Museum; p. 70 top National Library
of Wales, bottom National Museum of Wales (WFM); p. 71 left National Library of Wales,
right Welsh Industrial and Maritime Museum; p. 72 Merthyr Tydfil Heritage Trust; p. 73 left
Cyfarthfa Castle Art Gallery and Museum, right National Library of Wales; p. 74 National
Library of Wales; p. 75 top London Borough of Lambeth Archives Department, bottom left
National Library of Wales, bottom right Jeffrey F. Morgan with the kind permission of the
WFM; p. 77 top National Library of Wales, bottom Anthony Maddox; p. 78 bottom left Jeffrey
F. Morgan/Western Mail & Echo Ltd., top right Boxing News; p. 79 Western Mail & Echo
Ltd; p. 80 left Imperial War Museum, right National Library of Wales; p. 81 Imperial War
Museum; p. 82 Glynn Vivian Art Gallery; p. 83 top left National Library of Wales, bottom
right Colin Baglow; pp. 84, 86 and 87 top Gwynedd Archives and Museums Service; p. 87
bottom Welsh Industrial and Maritime Museum; p. 88 top and bottom Gwynedd Archives
and Museum Service, centre The National Trust p. 91 top Novosti Press Agency, bottom John
Massey Stewart; p. 92 top left Welsh Industrial and Maritime Museum, bottom left British
Steel, right Cardiff Workshops, East Moors; p. 93 Cardiff Workshops, East Moors; p. 94 top
STP Photography, bottom Jones + Brother; p. 95 left Mudiad Ysgolion Meithrin, right Inmos
Ltd.

Illustrations by Nick Hawken, Richard Hook, Andrew Howat, Christine Molan,
Tony Morris and Brian Walker.

Designers and Art Editors: John Brennan and Sarah Tyzack, Oxford
Picture Researcher: Rhian Ithel, Cardiff

Oxford University Press, Walton Street, Oxford OX2 6DP

Oxford   New York   Toronto
Delhi   Bombay   Calcutta   Madras   Karachi
Petaling Jaya   Singapore   Hong Kong   Tokyo
Nairobi   Dar es Salaam   Cape Town
Melbourne   Auckland

and associated companies in
Berlin and Ibadan

Oxford is a trade mark of Oxford University Press

Typeset by MS Filmsetting Limited, Frome, Somerset
Printed in Hong Kong   © Geraint H. Jenkins 1990   ISBN 0 19 917141 6

Contents

Time Chart

KING COAL'S REIGN BEGINS   1865

THE MIMOSA LEAVES FOR
PATAGONIA

1860s

1922

1926

1914-1918

THE GENERAL STRIKE

URDD GOBAITH
CYMRU

THE GREAT WAR

1930s

1936

1939-1945

THE SLUMP

BURNING THE
BOMBING-SCHOOL

THE SECOND
WORLD WAR

THE COLLEGE
BY THE SEA

1872

1886

THE TITHE WAR

1900 – 1903

THE QUARRYMEN'S
STRIKE

1904 – 1905

EVAN ROBERTS'S
RELIGIOUS REVIVAL

1913

THE SENGHENNYDD
DISASTER

1910

THE TONYPANDY RIOT

1962

THE WELSH LANGUAGE SOCIETY

1984 – 1985

THE MINERS' STRIKE

1

The Harvest-Mare

Let your imagination take you back to the year 1850. It's a hot sunny morning at the end of July. Over there in the big hay field is a laughing, joking crowd of men, women and children. The men are sharpening the long curved blades of their scythes on whetstones. Let's talk to one of the women.

'What's going on here?'

'Haymaking! We're going to cut all this hay. It should only take us until nightfall. A good man can cut an acre a day.'

'How is it done?'

'Why don't you stay and watch, then you'll know?' she laughs.

The men stand in a long line all along the edge of the field. One man gives the signal and they all begin to move forward, slicing down the hay with long sweeping strokes of their scythes. The women and children follow them. They work with their backs to the men and spread the mown hay in even layers over the field.

'Why are you spreading the hay out?'

She answers, but she doesn't stop working.

'To let it dry in the sun,' says the woman. 'We leave it here for a day or two, then we'll

Mowing hay with scythes

have to come back and turn it over. When it's dry we load it on to carts and take it to the farmer's barn. But it has to be dry. Wet hay would soon go rotten.'

'What do you do with the hay?'

'You don't know much about farming, do you? It's to feed the animals during the long winter months.'

'What if it rains?'

'We'll just have to pray that it won't. But it's not going to rain. We farmers know about the weather. We're in for a long dry spell.'

'There are a lot of people here.'

'Yes. Everybody helps with the harvest. It's our busiest time of the year. All the local people are here. The farmer gives them butter, cheese, and sacks of corn in payment. He even lets them plant their own potatoes in one of his fields. And when it's all over he gives us a big harvest supper.'

'When will the harvest be finished?'

'Oh, not for weeks yet. When the hay is in we have to cut the cereal crops. We cut the corn. Then we bind it into sheaves. Then they have to be dried and taken into the barns. We have great fun when the last of the corn is cut. Why don't you come back and see?'

Some weeks later we go back to our farm. The men have just finished cutting a huge corn field. All that is left is one tuft of corn. The rest is lying flat. The head reaper steps forward, kneels down and divides the tuft into three parts. He then plaits the pieces together. We wonder what's going to happen. Then the reapers sharpen their sickles and line up in a row about fifteen metres away from the last tuft of corn.

Starting with the head reaper, the labourers take it in turn to throw their sickles at the tuft to see who will be the first to cut it. Everybody cheers them on. Seven try – and fail! The eighth reaper spits on his fingers, takes a deep breath and hurls the sickle. It whizzes swiftly just above the ground and slashes through the tuft of corn. Everybody cheers. The victor then sings a little rhyme:

> 'Early in the morning I tracked her,
> In the evening I followed her,
> I've had her, I've had her.'

Nobody quite knows the meaning of the rhyme but it has been said for years and years. Now the fun really begins. The winner has to run with the plaited tuft back to the farm-house. He has to keep it dry. The maids and their friends from the farms around do their best to soak him by throwing buckets and pans of water at the harvest-mare. The victor dodges and weaves and finally reaches the farmhouse kitchen. He sighs with relief. His reward is a place of honour at the harvest supper and plenty of beer to drink! Had the maids managed to drench the mare, he would have been placed at the end of the table and made fun of all night. Meanwhile, the tuft – called *y gaseg fedi* (the harvest-mare) – is hung on a beam in the kitchen until the next harvest.

Thatching corn stacks

Farmer Careful

This is the story of John and Jane Careful of Cilhaul Uchaf, a small farm on the bleak, wet moorlands of mid-Wales. John and Jane were tenants of the powerful Williams Wynn family of Wynnstay, and they had six children. Life was a struggle. It was difficult to make ends meet. In an average year John's farm earned him £185. But incoming bills for rates, rents, tithes and taxes came to £220, which meant that the family was always in debt. When John told his landlord's steward how difficult things were, the steward replied: 'Improve your farm.' For the next three years John, Jane and the children did their best to make the farm more efficient, clean and tidy. The steward complimented them on their hard work and then, much to John's dismay, told them that he now planned to increase the rent by 35%. The family's worries deepened when the tithe-valuer called by. A tithe-valuer was a man who estimated what each farmer must pay the Church. He counted all the geese, pigs and sheep on the farm and then told Farmer Careful that he was doubling his tithe payment. To make things even worse, three land-valuers arrived, congratulated the farmer on his hard work, and promptly raised his rates by £9.

Naturally, Farmer Careful felt that this was unfair. He complained loudly in the village about the behaviour of greedy stewards, parsons and land-valuers. One of the steward's friends overheard him and reported his words to the steward. Within a few days a letter arrived from the landlord telling Farmer Careful to watch his step.

A few weeks later a rich young gentleman from London told John's landlord that he would very much like a farm for himself and

The title page of *Farmer Careful* by Samuel Roberts

FARMER CAREFUL

OF

CIL-HAUL UCHAF,

A BRIEF HISTORY OF WRONGS DONE TO HIS FAMILY; SHOWING THE NECESSITY FOR

REFORMS AS TO LAND MANAGEMENT;

AND A FEW SUGGESTIONS AS TO

IMPROVEMENTS,

BY

SAMUEL ROBERTS.

R. E. JONES, PRINTER AND STATIONER, CONWAY.

his newly-married wife. The steward was informed and was delighted to receive a couple of fine partridges and a pound of tea from the gentleman. He wrote back to say he was pretty sure that a local tenant would soon vacate his farm.

Farmer Careful was called to the steward's office and told off for complaining about the terms of his tenancy. The farmer replied that he and his family had to work hard from dawn to dusk in order to improve the farm. None of them had ever smoked, drunk alcohol, or wasted a single penny. But the steward refused to listen and handed him a notice to quit Cilhaul Uchaf. Farmer Careful returned home with tears in his eyes. His wife and children were bewildered, and didn't know what to say or do. The farmer's eldest son was furious and said that Welsh tenants were treated as badly as Russian serfs. He called all landlords 'bare-faced daylight robbers', and urged the rest of the family to emigrate to America. Farming a rich piece of land in Missouri was a much better prospect than suffering under robbers and thieves in Wales. And so, having been cheated and thrown off his farm, Farmer Careful and his family went in search of justice and freedom in America.

The story of Farmer Careful is based on the life of Samuel Roberts of Llanbryn-mair, Montgomeryshire. Known as 'S.R.', he lived for over fifty years in what he called a 'wet, cold, stony, bramble-bush' farm. He helped his father to run the farm. When his father died he took over the tenancy. He knew, therefore, how badly tenant-farmers were treated by landlords, stewards, tithe-collectors and tax-gatherers. Although his own father had done his best to improve his farm, he was tossed out of his property with no compensation. Many other poor farmers were badly treated in this way. Samuel Roberts was brave enough to speak out against the injustice. By preaching in chapels and writing to newspapers he campaigned on behalf of the welfare and rights of poor tenant-farmers. Between 1824 and 1885 he published nearly ninety books and pamphlets. He called for justice for tenant-farmers, votes for women, and an end to war, cruelty and oppression. When he died, aged 85, in September 1885, 'S.R.' was a household name in Wales.

Samuel Roberts

1

The Farm Labourer

As we've seen, life was hard for the tenant-farmer. But it was even more wretched for the farm labourer. The government wanted to find out what life was like for working people. Farm labourers were invited to speak to a committee of government inspectors between the years 1892 and 1894. Let's hear what David Davies, a farm labourer from Llangybi in Caernarfonshire had to say.

'I've been a farm labourer for nearly forty years. I was first hired when I was twelve and I've worked on dozens of different farms for six-monthly periods since then. I get up at five in the morning and finish work around eight at night. I have to plough, thatch, drain, hedge and milk in all kinds of weather. It's no wonder I suffer from aching bones, especially when the weather is damp.

'Labourers like me are only allowed into the farmhouse at meal-times. We eat very plain food. For breakfast we have wheaten bread and tea or milk. The bread is much better nowadays than it used to be. Barley bread was so tough you had to chew it for ages before swallowing it. I like the new wheaten bread. Mind you, we only get a thin smear of butter on it. At mid-day we come in from the fields for dinner. I only get fifteen minutes to gobble my food. It's usually potatoes and salted meat. The meat has often been kept for a year or so, and

it's almost too hard to chew. Farmers and labourers don't often eat fresh meat, and when they do it's usually a cow's head or a pig's head. The only dead cow we eat is the one the farmer can't sell to the butcher. If the cow is a good one, it's always sold to pay the rent. At five in the afternoon we have tea, bread and butter and oatmeal. Only rarely do we eat vegetables, and we never have fresh fruit. I'm sorry to say the farmer's food is not of the best.

'When I was much younger I used to sleep in lofts above the cattle. At one time there were five of us sleeping in the loft – and there were only three beds! There was hardly room to breathe and we often complained that the farmer looked after the cattle better than us. Rooms in the hay or stable loft were cold and draughty in winter, and hot and stuffy in the summer. Things got so bad that in the end I decided I'd rather walk miles after work to sleep in a proper room than share buildings with animals.

Farm labourers

Pig-killing at Llannarth, Dyfed, in the early twentieth century

Hand-milking in the open air

'I work long hours for very small wages. Wages tend to vary from place to place. At the moment I earn twelve shillings a week, and it's hard to feed and clothe my family properly. We haven't any money put aside in case of illness. If I fall sick we'll have to rely on charity. But lots of us would rather die of starvation than go to live in the workhouse. I'm ashamed that my small children go around barefoot in summer, and wear shabby wooden clogs in winter.

'Scores of labourers have had to leave their parishes for the ironworks and coal mines of South Wales. Most of them would have liked to have stayed here and bought some land. There's plenty of unused land here, but it's owned by the big landowners. None of them, unless they're up to their eyes in debt, will part with an acre, and they wouldn't dream of building decent cottages for farm labourers. All we want is a small plot of ground, a house and a garden. But we're slaves to the farmers and the landlords, and there's no one to campaign for our rights. Ap Ffarmwr, a journalist who writes in *Y Werin* (*The People*), urges us to set up unions of our own. Perhaps that will happen some day. But at the moment I live in dread of illness and old age. What will become of my family? I'm too old to join the 'coal rush' to South Wales, but my sons are sure to look for their El Dorado as soon as they're old enough to move away. It's sad, but who can blame them?'

Old and New Methods of Farming

Life was difficult for Welsh farmers. So much was against them: heavy rain, snow, ice, poor, acidic soil, poor drainage, and a lack of money to make improvements. Poor farmers could not afford new and efficient farm machinery and continued to use ancient tools and out-dated methods.

Old Ways

Ploughing with horses

Above: a reaping party in 1918

Left: hand-milking

Right: a hand-propelled seed-drill

By the end of the nineteenth century things were beginning to change in Wales. People were inventing new types of farm machinery. Those Welsh farmers who could afford to, began to buy the new machines, use new varieties of seeds, and use artificial fertilizers.

New Ways

A modern tractor ploughing

A combine harvester

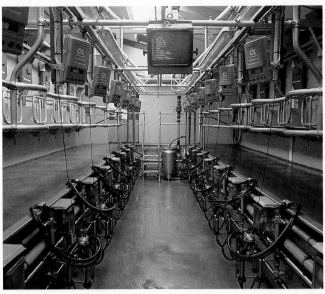

A herring-bone milking parlour

A modern seed-drill

A tractor and baler at work

The Village Craftsmen

Village craftsmen

We live in an age when household goods, utensils, clothes – all the things we need, in fact – are produced at great speed in factories. Large stores, hypermarkets and shops supply us with everything. Many products are shipped in from faraway places like Thailand and Japan. If something we buy is unsatisfactory we can complain and change it. Things were very different in the nineteenth century. In those days the needs of country folk were supplied by country craftsmen. Craftsmen were very skilful men who spent long hours preparing useful, long-lasting and beautiful products. They produced everything from farm tools and implements, household utensils and furniture, to clothes, boots and clogs. In the village of New Quay in Cardiganshire in 1851, there were eighteen carpenters and joiners, eight blacksmiths, six masons, six tailors, nine shoemakers and cobblers, and three weavers.

Some craftsmen used to travel from farm to farm, offering their services or selling their wares. Carpenters and cabinet-makers made furniture, saddlers produced harnesses, and turners and coopers made utensils for the kitchen and dairy. Wheelwrights, carpenters and blacksmiths produced gates, ploughs, wheels, shovels and horseshoes, while cobblers and clogmakers made shoes, boots and clogs. Let's look more closely at the work of some of them.

The blacksmith was a key figure. He didn't just make horseshoes and shoe horses. He fixed iron to cart axles, and hinges on gates. He made ploughs, harrows, hooks, nails and blades – anything you might need or ask for. As he prepared to shoe a horse, his first task was to remove the old shoes, file down the hooves, and measure each hoof in turn. He then heated rods of iron in a glowing fire and beat them into shape. Can you imagine the sparks flying? He then drove nail holes into the iron before carefully fitting the shoe to the hoof.

Some communities could boast special craftsmen. At Aber-cuch in north Pembroke-shire skilful wood-turners were famous for making trenchers, ladles, spoons, bowls, tubs and milking-stools. A trencher is a sort of wooden plate. In the days when there were no products made of enamel, tin, china and plastic, people used to eat and drink from wooden bowls.

The turner liked to use wood from the sycamore tree because it was so strong and clean. When making a wooden bowl he used a treadle lathe in order to make the bowl revolve. He then used a gouge and a chisel to shape the bowl. Wooden spoons for eating *cawl* (broth) were very popular, as were larger spoons and ladles for use in the kitchen. The turner used to sell his wares in local fairs and markets.

An unusual group of craftsmen were the cloggers. They cut soles for clogs worn by labourers, farmers, miners, textile workers and children. Clogs were thick, heavy shoes which were ideal for muddy fields and waterlogged mines. Cloggers travelled in groups around the country in search of alder or beech trees. They cut down the trees and sawed the trunks into logs of different sizes. Each log was then split into blocks. Using a special knife, the clogger then cut the soles into different shapes so that they could be made to fit men, women or children. The soles were then stacked in the open air to dry before being sent off to factories in the north of England where the clogs were made in workshops.

There are very few specialist craftsmen in Wales nowadays. Most goods are either made in factories in towns and cities, or are imported from abroad. Modern technology has almost made the skills of these craftsmen things of the past. But you can still find some people who carry on these old crafts at the National Folk Museum in St. Fagans, near Cardiff.

Shoeing a horse

A bowl turner's stall

Travelling clog sole cutters

The Woollen Industry

The Dobcross power loom could produce lengths of cloth in yard widths

How many places can you think of in Wales which include the word *pandy*? The name tells us that at some time there was a woollen mill nearby. Today there are few of these mills still working, but if we were to go back to the early twentieth century we would find many of them in the rural areas of Wales. Let's try to find out what life was like in a woollen mill community in 1913.

We have come to a small village called Dre-fach Felindre in the Teifi Valley, in north Carmarthenshire. Many people living in the villages around the Teifi Valley work in the woollen mills. There are spinners, stocking knitters, weavers, carders, dyers and fullers. Let's talk to David Lewis, the owner of the Cambrian Mill – one of the largest. Mr. Lewis is very proud of his new factory.

'I began in a small and very shabby weaving shop but decided to invest money in building the fine new factory you see before you. It was hard going at first but I found there was an ever increasing demand for the cloth we make.

Calico loom

I'm now able to employ more than fifty local people. We used to depend on water as a source of power for our machines but now we've got modern gas engines.

'Building this factory was a great risk but we were helped by two things. First of all the railway line was built. This meant we could get goods we produced to markets much more quickly and sell our cloth at more or less the same price as products from places like Yorkshire.'

'*What is the other reason for your success?*'

'Well, our speciality is good Welsh flannel and we sell large quantities of it. There's a huge demand for it, especially from the coal miners in South Wales. The miners all wear flannel vests, you know, and the women seem to like it for bedclothes and shawls.'

We thank Mr. Lewis for his help and ask if we can talk to some of his workers. In the mill the sound is deafening. We see a boy near one of the machines and ask him to tell us something about his work.

'I'm 14 years old and work for 12 hours each day, for six days each week. For this I'm paid 10 pence a day. That is not as much as most of my friends can earn on a farm. But at least I am sure of a job throughout the year.'

The teazle gig was used to raise the 'nap' on cloth

At this point his young brother comes over to talk to us. He is only ten years old and works for three hours each evening and five hours on Saturday. He tells us that his mother regularly takes shawls and blankets home to hem and fringe over the weekend.

Despite the hard work everybody seems to be happy. They enjoy living in a small village like Dre-fach where they know everybody. Besides, there are plenty of things to do. A brass band has recently been started and there is a local male voice choir, a billiards hall, and a football team.

This type of garment could have been woven in 1860. The pattern of red and black stripes became popular one hundred years earlier.

What is left of the Dre-fach mills today? Like most of the woollen mills of Wales they were forced to close after the First World War as demand for Welsh flannel declined. They found they could no longer compete with cloths produced cheaply in other countries, and many young people preferred lighter cloths to thick Welsh flannel. Sadly, our Cambrian factory was burned down in 1919 and most of the three-storey building was destroyed.

The fire at the mill

In recent years, however, the damage has been repaired and the Cambrian factory has become the home of the Museum of the Welsh Woollen Industry. You will find there old mill buildings, a water wheel, machinery, hand-tools, and displays of carding, spinning, and hand-loom weaving.

Thousands of visitors flock to the Museum each year. Why don't you join them? You'll be made very welcome and are bound to learn a lot about what life was like in a woollen mill all those years ago.

The Cambrian factory today

Farmers Protest

It is Sunday morning, 29 October, 1876. We've joined a group of tenant-farmers riding on horseback to Llwynrhydowen chapel in south Cardiganshire. They're dressed in their Sunday best and as we trot along they tell us about their troubles. One of them is very bitter:

'There's no justice to be had in Wales. The big landlords own all the land, while we have to work our fingers to the bone to make a living. They tell me that the Earl of Lisburne owns over 42,000 acres up at Trawsgoed, and here I am trying to grow enough food to feed my wife and children on a poor farm of 35 acres.'

Another farmer agrees:

'They don't just want land. They also want the power to tell us how to vote, and where to worship. Many of our friends have suffered because they voted against their landlord's candidate in the parliamentary elections held eight years ago. Stewards threw them off their farms and had the cheek to claim they were poor farmers. Many of them went to America, and I don't blame them. I was turned out of my farm and forced to live in a tiny cottage. I have to bend double to get through my front door, but I'd rather bend there than bend before any cruel landlords. I'll never give in to them.'

Another farmer joins in:

'We're on our way to a protest meeting at our chapel. Last week our chapel secretary received a letter from the steward of Allt-yr-odyn estate. We lease the chapel and burial ground from the owner of Allt-yr-odyn. The letter ordered us to close the chapel and graveyard. That's their way of punishing us for daring to defy them.'

As we approach Llwynrhydowen chapel we can see that hundreds of people have

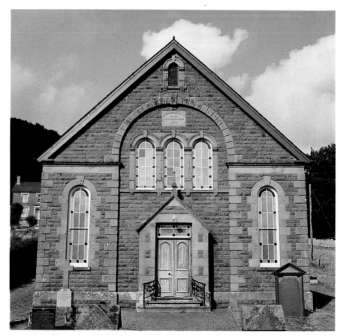

The new chapel at Llwynrhydowen

gathered at the crossroads nearby. There are farmers, craftsmen, labourers and their wives. Many people have ridden or walked several miles to support local chapel-goers. People are weeping openly as they gaze at the padlocks on the chapel door, and on the graveyard gate. No one can get into the chapel to worship, or visit the graves of loved-ones. Our fellow travellers are furious and are about to break the locks when the minister of the chapel steps forward. The crowd falls silent as he climbs the steps outside the entrance to the graveyard. He turns to face them.

This is Gwilym Marles, minister of the Unitarian chapels of Llwynrhydowen and Bwlchyfadfa. His real name is William Thomas and he was born nearby in Llanybydder. Although his health is poor, he is a tall and handsome man, with an impressive black beard. Everyone respects him because he is a poet and a schoolmaster as well as a minister. He is well-liked by tenant-farmers because he speaks his mind fearlessly. On election days he has always spoken against greedy landlords and cruel stewards. Gwilym Marles holds up his arms and begins to speak:

'My dear friends. This deed has been done to damage all of us. They know I'm a poor man with a large family, and they want to silence me. But I'm not afraid of them. As long as you remain faithful to me, and as long as I remain faithful to God, we will succeed.'

The crowd listens silently, then claps loudly as Gwilym Marles steps down. Although the people are angry and bitter, they decide not to break the padlocks. Instead they begin to collect money to build a new chapel.

Local newspapers helped the people of Llwynrhydowen to win support for their cause. A few weeks later, in time for Christmas, a small wooden chapel had been built. People could worship there for the time being. But a much bigger chapel was planned. It was

eventually completed in October 1879. By then Gwilym Marles was a very sick man. He died, aged 45, on 11 December, 1879 and was buried in front of the new chapel. He had inspired his flock to set an example to landlords as well as their fellow men. Inside the new chapel there is a tablet in his memory. On it are these words:

'A man full of God's gifts in his sermons,
and his heart on fire on behalf of
the freedom and all the goodness of man.'

Gwilym Marles

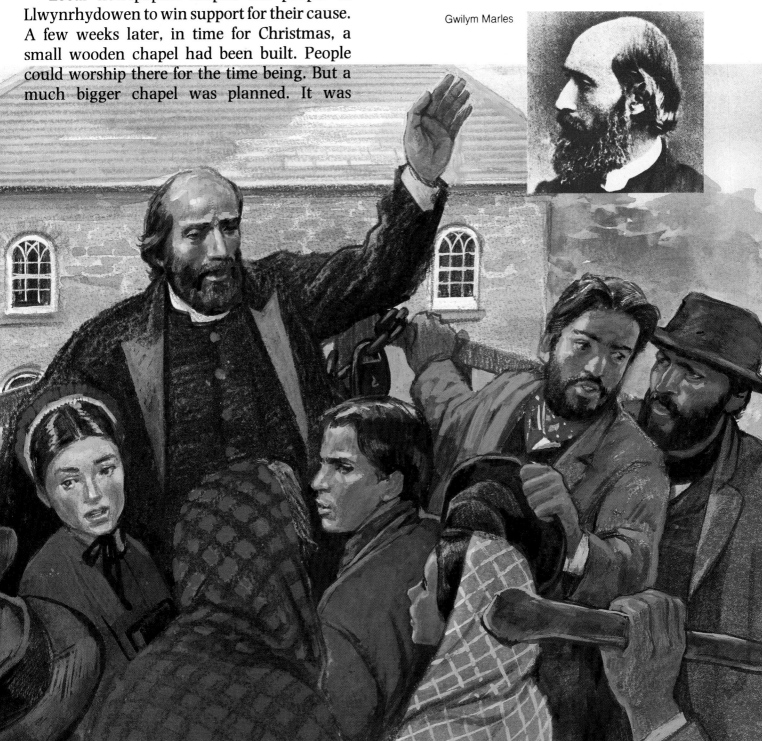

The Tithe War

Thomas Gee on Degwm

Elsewhere in Wales at this time farmers were protesting because they were still forced to pay tithes to the Church. A tithe was a tenth part of the farmer's annual produce. The amount a farmer had to pay in tithes was based on the value of the land he rented, the food his farm produced, and the price of oats, wheat and barley. When the price of corn and cattle fell dramatically, farmers couldn't afford to pay tithes. They also said that since they were chapel-goers they should not be expected to pay for the upkeep of the Church. 'Pay no tithes to an alien Church' was their slogan. In 1886 a 'Tithe War' broke out in the Vale of Clwyd in Denbighshire.

Farmers couldn't afford to pay tithes and begged local clergymen to reduce tithe payments. Some clergymen agreed to help, but others refused. When they refused, farmers received a notice demanding payment within ten days. If the farmer had no money, bailiffs were sent to his home to take away animals and goods which were then auctioned to raise the tithe money. Farmers formed angry protest movements at cattle auctions. They shouted insults, waved sticks, threw eggs and stones, and jostled bailiffs. During some sales confiscated cattle were soaped and greased so that the bailiffs couldn't handle them. Crowds of protesters heckled, hooted and hissed whenever auctioneers called for bids.

Thomas Gee, editor of the famous newspaper *Baner ac Amserau Cymru*, formed the Anti-Tithe League, a society to protect the rights of farmers. Gee urged poets to send in songs to encourage the protesters, and to make fun of the Church. He even called his own horse *Degwm* (Tithe). Feelings were running high as farmers cried 'No more tithes!' and

'Down with the Church!'

In the summer of 1887 serious riots broke out at Llangwm. The local parson Ellis Roberts (Elis Wyn o Wyrfai) had agreed to reduce tithe payments by 10%, but the Church Commissioners refused to allow him to do so. Bailiffs were sent into the Llangwm area to confiscate animals at four farms. A sale of the confiscated animals was arranged. At three in the morning, on 25 May, twenty-five policemen set off from Denbigh to make sure there was no trouble. When they arrived at Llangwm at six, they were met by Ap Mwrog, the auctioneer, Edward Vaughan, the valuer, and Amos Maltby, a butcher.

The farmers of Llangwm were waiting for them. When the policemen were spotted, horns were sounded and guns fired in order to warn other farmers. Soon a large and hostile crowd had gathered. At Fron Isaf farm, two cows were put up for sale. But no one could hear the auctioneer's voice above the catcalls and boos. Eggs, cow dung and stones were thrown, and there were scuffles with the police. No bids were made for the cows, so the auctioneer sold them to Amos Maltby, the butcher. But when the butcher tried to move the cows, his way was blocked by a horse pulling a heavy roller. Angry and frustrated, the auctioneer, the valuer, the butcher, and the policemen left Llangwm empty-handed.

Two days later they returned in a large carriage. Look-outs had been posted and a crowd of three hundred people had assembled to surprise them. The road was deliberately blocked and the travellers in the carriage were showered with eggs and clods of turf. Horns and drums were sounded and the noise upset the horses so badly that they bolted. As the horses galloped away the carriage overturned and was badly damaged. One horse was severely injured and had to be destroyed at once. Fighting broke out as the crowd set upon the auctioneer and the valuer. Many of them wanted to throw Ap Mwrog into the river and leave him to drown. When he begged for mercy on his knees, the farmers' leaders forced him to sign a paper declaring that he would never return to Llangwm 'to sell for tithes'. He and his colleagues were forced to turn their coats inside out, to make them look stupid, and then were marched off to Corwen railway station followed by a laughing, jeering crowd. Later on, however, many rioters were arrested.

In July, thirty-one of the Llangwm rioters were brought before the Ruthin magistrates. The case was adjourned. Then it became known that the eight leaders had been summoned to appear in court in London, away from their supporters. Welsh Members of Parliament made such a fuss that, in the end, the eight leaders were tried at Ruthin on 28 February, 1888. The eight included five farmers, a draper, a grocer, and a preacher. By this time the local press had nicknamed them 'The Tithe Martyrs'. The judge dealt leniently with them and they were bound over to keep the peace.

Other riots followed in the Vale of Clwyd and spread to many other parts of Wales. Thomas Gee urged farmers to be brave and stubborn, and money was raised to help those who had suffered. Eventually, the 'Tithe War' was won. In 1891 Parliament passed an Act ordering the landlords, rather than their tenants, to pay tithes. After that, things quietened down.

A cartoon of the time

Two Welsh Farmers

Imagine that you're a reporter working for a London newspaper. Your editor has told you to travel to Wales to write a story about the problems facing Welsh farmers today. A dairy farmer in Dyfed welcomes you.

'Why do you look so worried?' you ask.

'I feel badly cheated, and so do my neighbours. The milk quotas are to blame. I used to keep 75 dairy cows but now the authorities in Brussels say that I'm only allowed to keep 40 cows.'

You've done your homework before coming. You know that Brussels is the headquarters of the European Economic Commission (EEC). Britain is a member of the EEC. In 1984 the Commission decided that European farmers were producing too much milk. They told each farmer the maximum amount of milk he could produce. He mustn't produce more than that amount. This is his 'quota'.

'Up until 1984 the government had been encouraging us to produce more and more milk. It was made easier for farmers to borrow money from the bank to buy more cows for our milk herds. Then came this bombshell. I don't mind telling you I'm up to my eyes in debt. I've spent thousands of pounds reseeding fields, buying new cattle, and building milking parlours. Once the quotas came in I had to reduce the number of cows on my farm and cut back in many other ways. Most farms in this area are dairy farms and I know of good farmers who've had to sell up and leave the area.'

'Are you saying that the quotas have caused a lot of suffering?'

'Yes. Scores of farmers are on the verge of bankruptcy. We've done our best to protest against the cuts. Some farmers protested by blocking main roads with tractors during the cyclists' Milk Race through Wales. Others went

Welsh dairy farmers protest

'You must have heard about the nuclear explosion at Chernobyl back in 1986. Well, even though it happened many, many miles away it's virtually ruined my life. A week after the explosion, contaminated rain, blown over in clouds from Russia, fell here. None of us knew at the time that our sheep were eating contaminated grass. Many farmers like me were stopped from selling lambs and slaughtering sheep. When the word got round butchers began putting up notices in their shops saying 'No Welsh lamb here'. We still don't know what the long-term effects will be on farming in Wales.'

'You live within fifteen miles of the nuclear power station at Trawsfynydd. Does that scare you?'

'Yes. We call the power station Trawsobyl. I'm sure my family has been contaminated by radiation from the plant. I know the experts say the place is safe and that it gives work for 600 people, but we suspect that the risks to our health are great. Trawsfynydd lake is full of caesium and you'd be daft to fish for trout there. I don't care what the scientists say, I'm certain that the land and people around here are being poisoned. There's a dark cloud hanging over our heads and I fear for the future of our children.'

to Cardiff and left a cow's head on the steps of the Welsh Office. I remember the wives of some farmers (not mine though!) bathing in milk on the streets of Carmarthen. But nobody took any notice. That's why so many farms are now up for sale.'

'Have the cuts in milk production affected other people in this area?'

'Yes, they have. They've affected those who sell cattle food, fertilizers and machinery. Slaughter houses and haulage firms have much less work. Local creameries have been closed down and, because so many people are out of work, local shops have been badly hit. Young Welsh-speaking people are leaving to look for jobs in towns and cities in England. This affects the future of the Welsh language and local Welsh-speaking schools. You can tell your readers that our whole way of life is under threat. Soon Wales will be full of retired English people, hippies, and rich foreigners buying holiday homes. If you don't believe me, drive on to North Wales and ask my cousin what he thinks.'

The farmer gives you the name and address of his cousin. He is a sheep farmer in Merioneth. When you arrive he tells you he has 400 sheep and lambs grazing on rather poor mountain land. He seems even more gloomy than his cousin. You ask him why.

Trawsfynydd power station

23

Emigration to America

America in the nineteenth century was a very large new country with a very small population. The American government wanted more people to come and live there. Many Welsh families left for America. Farmers were driven to leave by the poverty of their farms and the cruelty of their landlords. They were encouraged to settle in places like Ohio, Iowa and Illinois where land was available. Skilled industrial workers emigrated to the cities of Scranton and Wilkes-Barre where they could earn high wages as coal miners and steel-workers. Posters and books told the Welsh how splendid America was. Letters were sent back to Wales telling relatives what the New World had to offer. Some of these letters have survived in family papers or printed newspapers.

Although many people were tempted by the rich and new way of life which America offered, it wasn't easy to break family ties. It meant leaving loved-ones like parents or grandparents behind. The journey itself, in small, overcrowded ships, was long and dangerous. Let's see what some of the emigrants say. Here is what John Lloyd wrote in 1868 in a letter to his parents who lived near St. Asaph:

As we have seen, in Wales there were too many poor tenants and too few farms. It wasn't easy to earn a decent living on the poor soils of upland Wales. To them, America was a rich and fertile land where a man could stand on his own feet. This is what a Welshman called William wrote to his parents, brothers and sisters, in 1856:

> I am sure that there is no more fertile land in creation than in the state of Iowa. It produces its crops without the need of manure. It contains from five to twenty-five feet of rich black earth. It is easy to farm. After ploughing it once, it is like a garden and they can raise anything on it. It is a healthy country and it is cheap. The price of land from the government is about 5s. 3d. in your money. Here you get it for less than a year's rent in Wales. One crop is enough to pay for the land. You urge me to come back to the Old Country. But my adopted country is better than the land of my birth.

> HA! HA! Here I am at last with my feet on the famous land of America. Many laughed at me when I said I was coming here and said, "We'll believe you when you've gone." Well, will they believe me now because I have gone. I left Liverpool at 6 o'clock in the afternoon on Tuesday 16 June on board the steamship Manhattan. My bed was a long narrow shell and we lay in rows along it like red herrings. As we neared Newfoundland we saw great icebergs which made the weather much colder. We, the Welsh got together and held a small school, reading the Bible.

> The entrance to New York is so fine that it makes any man's heart leap with happiness.
> Large steamboats are seen going to and fro on the river. For curiosity I went aboard one and, heavens alive! the first thing I saw was a barber's shop and a Negro busily shaving some friend. There are quite a number of Welsh but they are all scattered.

For some emigrants, however, loneliness and disappointment lay ahead. Some of those who went to work in the coal, iron and steel industries of Pennsylvania were badly affected by strikes, depression and falling wages. To them, America was not a paradise. Thomas Morris, writing from the town of Providence in Pennsylvania, told his brothers and sisters of his experiences:

> While I was in Wales, I heard much talk of the high wages in America. That was what brought me from Old Wales to get my share of them. But oh! me! before I reached land the wheel had turned. Wages were continually being lowered and still are. We have had two decreases since I came here.
>
> Coal is dropping in the market. There are too many men in the country connected with coal mining. They are almost treading on each other in these parts. I hear that many of my old neighbours intend coming over this summer. Let them be patient, lest they be sorry that they come to the American Wilderness.

Many Welsh emigrants naturally took their language and culture with them and did their best to resist American ways. But by 1890, when over 100,000 Welsh people had settled in America, most of them had become English-speaking Americans. The Welsh lost their Welshness in the prairies and cities of America. It was with great sadness that the Rev. D. S. Davies said this in a letter to John Thomas of Merthyr, in 1872:

> Large-scale emigration has been a loss to our nation and to the Welsh language. Everything here destroys our common heritage. Many of those who emigrate here from Wales join the English. The result is that Welsh causes do not flourish in America. There is not one Welsh bookstore in the country nor a Welsh public library. We have perhaps 400 Welsh chapels in different States, but the English are taking over many of them. The Welsh language has no prospect of success in this country.

Above: An emigration poster
Right: Immigrants on the
S.S. Patricia in 1906

Patagonia

This is the port of Liverpool on the twenty-fifth of May, 1865. Hundreds of people have gathered together at the quayside to wave goodbye to 163 brave Welsh emigrants. 56 married adults, 32 single men, 12 single women, a widower and 62 children have boarded a tea-clipper weighing 447 tons. Most of the men on board are colliers and farmers from South Wales. Everyone cheers when the Red Dragon of Wales is hoisted to the mast-head. To further loud cheers, the ship moves off slowly. But then, unexpectedly, it drops anchor and three days go by before the ship is ready to sail. By then, most of the watching crowd have gone home! This was the bungled beginning of one of the most brave and romantic episodes in the history of Wales.

The tea-clipper, called the *Mimosa*, was on its way to Patagonia in South America. The dream of Michael D. Jones, a chapel minister and a fervent Welsh patriot, was coming true. Michael D. Jones's dream was to set up a Welsh colony across the waters. At first he thought that the State of Oregon would be an ideal place for Welsh people. But he was afraid that the Welsh would soon lose their language and culture in America. Somewhere much further away would suit them better. As it happened, the Argentine government was trying to tempt people from Europe to settle in South America.

Michael D. Jones was excited by the idea. He hoped that Welsh colonists would set up chapels and schools of their own and live in peace and freedom. No longer would the Welsh be slaves to cruel landlords in their native land.

Michael D. Jones began collecting money to pay for the journey. Lewis Jones, a printer from Caernarfon, travelled to Buenos Aires to discuss setting up the Welsh colony with the Argentine government. Adverts placed in newspapers offered a passage to South America for as little as £12. Children could travel at half price. But many people claimed it was a risky venture. Others said that the Welsh had a duty to stay at home to fight for their language and freedom.

Exactly two months after leaving Liverpool, the *Mimosa* arrived at the bay known today as Puerto Madryn. Although two babies had died at sea, the journey had been fairly smooth. The real problems lay ahead! Before sailing, few people had imagined what life would really be like in South America. It was the middle of winter when they arrived. The passengers gazed miserably at the grey mountains and rocky slopes. Was this the paradise they had been promised?

When they landed, the Welsh were shocked to find the soil so dry and barren. For the first six weeks they had to live and sleep in caves. But they were keen to learn more about this strange land. When the weather improved they travelled by boat to their destination – the lower Chubut Valley. There they began the work of clearing the land. The Argentine government helped by sending them food. The local Indians taught them to hunt. Slowly but surely, the small band of Welsh colonists began to master the elements. A chapel, a school and a prison were built. A Welsh newspaper was printed, and eisteddfodau and singing festivals were held. A second Welsh settlement, called Cwm Hyfryd (Pleasant Valley), was set up at the foot of the Andes mountains.

Cwm Hyfryd, Patagonia, by the artist Kyffin Williams

Michael D. Jones's aim had been to send 30,000 emigrants to Patagonia. But by the end of 1875 only 700 Welsh people had settled there. There wasn't enough money to support the scheme properly. Since the colony was so far away it was difficult to organize things properly from Wales. Soon, Spaniards and Italians began to arrive and the Welsh were unable to keep themselves apart from other races and languages. From 1896 onwards Welsh children were taught Spanish in schools. Michael D. Jones's dream of a Welsh-speaking colony faded.

Today, most of those who still speak Welsh in Patagonia are old people. Spanish is the first language of young children. By the end of the twentieth century the Welsh language will probably have disappeared from Patagonia. But the heroic story of those brave Welsh colonists who travelled 7,000 miles to South America will never be forgotten.

Michael D. Jones

Thomas Gee's Gwyddoniadur

John has been told by his teacher to prepare a special project on old Welsh books. He is fortunate to have parents who sell second-hand books. As he browses among some of the old and rather dusty books in his parents' shop he comes across ten fat volumes. It looks to him like an old set of encyclopaedias. He opens volume six and begins to read about a famous preacher called John Jones, Tal-y-sarn. When he was a boy, John Jones used to preach sermons to the ducks on his farm.

As the young boy preached, he sometimes waved his hand towards them. His listeners, expecting food from his hand, applauded him noisily. This pleased the preacher. But eventually his audience decided that this was a pretty poor sermon. They began to quack loudly and drowned the preacher's voice. He said, 'Oh! my little people, it's too early to start singing. I haven't finished my sermon yet and we usually pray before we sing.'

John grins and turns over the pages. There are sections on animals and birds, poets and scholars. He finds coloured maps of China and Italy. The lives of famous men like Alexander the Great, Leonardo da Vinci and Napoleon are recorded. How many people, John wonders, know that Abraham was born in 1996 BC? John wishes there were more colour photographs in these volumes. The print is small and, as he reads on, he begins to doze. Soon he's fast asleep and dreaming. In his dream John finds himself in the printing house of Thomas Gee in Denbigh. In Mr. Gee's office the calendar on the wall tells him that it is March 1879. Mr. Gee greets him gruffly.

'Ah! You're the young man who's curious about my set of encyclopaedias *Y Gwyddoniadur*! There's never been anything like it before in Welsh. Even the *Western Mail* has called it "the King of Welsh books". We're publishing the tenth and last volume this month. The first volume came out twenty-five years ago, so you can see it's been a major task. But when that last volume is bound there'll be 7,517 pages in print. What do you think of that?'

Before John can reply, Mr. Gee grabs his arm and marches him down to the printing works.

'Welsh readers can't get enough of this stuff. I sell the encyclopaedia in instalments in shops, workshops and on the streets. Even the poorest folk save their pennies to buy Gee's *Gwyddoniadur*. They've got no idea of the problems involved in publishing a work of this size. I have to keep writers, editors, printers, binders and booksellers on their toes. Their wages have to be paid. And then there's supplies of paper, ink and type to buy. It's a good job my father taught me the tricks of the trade. Although I say it myself, I'm a good businessman. I'll use every good idea I can – as long as it's profitable!'

Mr. Gee ushers John into the printing works. The noise is deafening. Four large printing machines are throbbing away. Mr. Gee's employees jump to attention when they see their master.

'You see these men? They're proud to work for the most famous publisher in North Wales. They work hard for me because they know I work hard for them. I'm the boss here and everyone has to obey my commands. That's the only way to run a business properly. None of *my* workers belongs to a union. They're happy enough to work sixty hours a week because they're well paid and well looked after here.'

Mr. Gee shows John the final instalment of *Y Gwyddoniadur* on the press.

'All type is set by hand here. I pay the compositors half a crown a page. We use a process called stereotyping when we're print-ing. When the type is set we make a cast of it in plaster of Paris. This enables us to keep the work intact and reprint it when we've sold off the edition. We usually run off around 6,000 copies of *Y Gwyddoniadur*, and they sell like hot cakes. I know you'd like to see more colour

plates in them. But illustrations are very ex-pensive and I have to buy them from English publishers. You have to remember that I've got other things to do as well. Most of my profits come from jobbing work – printing invoices, letterheads, time-tables, billheads, trade cards – that kind of thing. And I'm sure you know I'm the editor of *Baner ac Amserau Cymru*, the most popular Welsh newspaper of our day. I sell up to 50,000 copies of *Y Faner* every week. What do you think of that?'

Before John can reply, Mr. Gee ushers him back to his office. Mr. Gee wants to get on with his work. But first he brings out a handsome volume.

'Here's a gift to help you remember this visit. It's a de-luxe volume of *Y Gwyddoniadur*, bound in extra morocco with gilt edges. Read it, young man, and learn from it.'

When John wakes up he finds that the old dusty volume on his lap has vanished. In its place is a brand new, expensive version of *Y Gwyddoniadur*, the most popular encyclopaedia in nineteenth-century Wales.

Right: A colour plate from the encyclopaedia

Below: Thomas Gee's employees

The National Eisteddfod

Llew Llwyfo

Someone once said that only the Welsh people would ever have thought of putting up a huge tent in the middle of a wet, muddy field and spending a whole week walking around it! He was referring to the National Eisteddfod of Wales, which is held every year during the first full week in August. For many Welsh-speakers, the Eisteddfod is the highlight of the year. It gives them the chance to speak Welsh for a whole week and to listen to poetry, literature and song. It also draws Welsh people home from all parts of the world. The Eisteddfod is a very special cultural festival which does

its best to foster the Welsh language. But that was not always the case.

Let's return to 1867 when the Eisteddfod was held in Carmarthen. A huge wooden pavilion, designed to house 7,000 people, was set up in a field outside the town. The pavilion cost £794 to put up.

Sawdust covered the grass indoors and important guests were given numbered seats. Those who organized the Eisteddfod insisted on the use of the English language in the pavilion. Their aim was to please the English-speaking visitors. Musicians, singers and entertainers were brought from London. Lectures and exhibitions were arranged. The manager of London Zoo gave a talk on snakes and serpents!

Ordinary people were very angry to hear so little Welsh spoken on the Eisteddfod platform. They jeered loudly when English, French, German and Italian music was played, and they called for popular Welsh songs. Outside the weather got steadily worse. As a plump lady called Madame Patey-Whytock sang *The Storm*, part of the pavilion roof flew off and rain poured in. Welsh folk were delighted and began calling for their own popular entertainers. Their favourite star was Lewis William Lewis, better known as Llew Llwyfo. Llew was a popular baritone who was the life and soul of concerts throughout Wales. The Welsh idolized him and they began to chant 'Llew! Llew!' as Madame Patey-Whytock struggled to finish her song.

The organizers of the Eisteddfod were furious. They believed that Llew Llwyfo was too common and coarse. Madame Patey-Whytock said he was 'a suitable specimen for a menagerie'. There were also other quarrels and disputes. The adjudicators of the Chair Poem failed to agree and a famous Welsh poet – Ceiriog – was called in to choose the winner. No wonder *The London Review* called the National Eisteddfod 'a yearly joke'. The organizers did little to help the Welsh language to survive. It was left to the small eisteddfodau, held in chapels and halls in villages and towns all over Wales, to hold their competitions in Welsh.

In some ways, the National Eisteddfod of today hasn't changed much since the 1860's. It is still held every year in North and South Wales in turn. A huge pavilion is erected in the middle of a field, and the cost of putting it up is still a major headache. And, of course, it nearly

A modern National Eisteddfod

always rains heavily during Eisteddfod week! But in other ways, great changes have happened. The most important change has been its growth in popularity. Tens of thousands of people attend every year. This means that everything has to be organized properly. There is now a full-time director and two organizers to make sure everything runs like clockwork. When the Eisteddfod was held at Porthmadog in 1987 the total cost was over a million pounds!

The Eisteddfod has also become a Welsh language event. From 1950 onwards Welsh has been the official language of the Eisteddfod. This 'Welsh Rule' has helped to keep the language and culture alive. There is special translation equipment for those who don't understand Welsh. The Welsh Learners' Tent is a very popular centre. Over 5,000 people pack into the main pavilion to watch the ceremonies when poets are crowned and chaired. Younger people, many of whom camp in tents, prefer to listen to live music played by their favourite rock groups and folk singers. Welsh books, records, cassettes and crafts are on sale in neatly grouped tents and stalls around the main pavilion. Llew Llwyfo would have enjoyed the colour, fun and pageantry of the modern Welsh Eisteddfod. He would probably be a television star today!

The College by the Sea

In Aberystwyth there is a university college. It is housed in a building on the sea-front. It's known as the 'College by the Sea'. But this fine building wasn't meant to be a college at all. It was supposed to be a hotel! It was built by Thomas Savin, a businessman from Oswestry. Savin had first made money as a draper, but later on he began to build railways. His great dream, however, was to turn the towns of Cardigan Bay into attractive seaside resorts. His favourite town was Aberystwyth and he hoped to make it 'the Brighton of Wales'.

In 1864 Thomas Savin bought a small triangular building called Castle House. His aim was to expand it and turn it into the biggest hotel in the kingdom. He hired J. P.

Seddon, an architect from London, and ordered him to draw up plans in a hurry. Savin said that he wanted the hotel completed by the following summer. 500 labourers and craftsmen were employed to build the hotel. They worked so quickly that the architect couldn't keep up with them! Perhaps that is why the hotel looked rather odd. Everything was going well until Thomas Savin suddenly went bankrupt. He had spent £80,000 on the Castle hotel. Now he had no choice but to sell the building.

The hotel was bought by Hugh Owen, a Welsh civil servant, and a group of his friends. They bought it for £10,000! But they had no intention of using the building as a hotel. For

years they had dreamed of founding a college in Wales. Welsh children who wanted to continue their education had to try for places in English universities. Owen wanted a Welsh college which would be as good as any university in the world.

But Hugh Owen and his business friends were also short of money. Their message to the Welsh people was 'Wake up to the need for education.' They set out to raise the money they needed. On the fifteenth of October, 1872, a public holiday was observed in Aberystwyth. All the shops were closed and there were flags and banners everywhere. Ninety important guests were invited to a banquet in the new college.

Hugh Owen

On the tables there were chickens, ducks, grouse, hams, partridges, pheasants, turkey and veal pies, as well as bowls of jelly and blancmange. Glasses were raised and the guests cried 'Success to the College!' In a speech, David Davies, the rich coalowner from Llandinam, promised to give £3,000 to the college to start the fund off.

There were only 26 students at first. Aged between 14 and 25, they lived in lodgings in the town. They were taught by four teachers, including the Principal, Thomas Charles Edwards. No longer would young Welsh people be forced to leave Wales to study.

But the future of the college at Aberystwyth was still in doubt. Lack of money was the main problem. Once more, Hugh Owen worked hard to raise funds. He travelled by rail to the towns and villages of Wales, pleading with people to donate money to the new Welsh college. Station-masters all over Wales came to

The old college by the sea

know Hugh Owen and his little black bag very well. His efforts inspired the ordinary people. Craftsmen, farmers, labourers, miners and quarrymen sent him every penny they could spare. Special collections were made in Welsh chapels. Over 100,000 people, from all over Wales, contributed pennies and shillings to help the 'College by the Sea'. Without the pennies of the poor, the college would never have survived.

The college at Aberystwyth has grown rapidly in recent years. It now has over 3,000 students, most of whom are taught in modern buildings on a fine campus overlooking the town. But Thomas Savin's 'hotel' still houses the Departments of Welsh, and Education. Special attention is given to Welsh language and culture, and it's good to know that the college library is named after Hugh Owen. But if things had turned out differently, the Hugh Owen Library might have easily been 'Thomas Savin's Banquet Hall'!

The new college campus

33

The Welsh Not

When he was nine years old, Owen Morgan Edwards was sent to school at Llanuwchllyn in Merioneth. Among the things he first noticed were the cold grey slates on the roof, the yellow and green paint on the walls, the wooden floors, and the cane on the teacher's desk! When he grew up he wrote about his experiences on that day:

'The word spread that a new child had come to school. Many cruel children eyed me closely. Most of them were cheeky children from the village. The teacher had told me quietly not to speak a word of Welsh. But then bad children did their utmost to make me shout. In the end they succeeded. I lost my temper. Everyone laughed. A piece of string, with a heavy block of wood, was placed around my neck ... That block of wood was placed around my neck hundreds of times after that ... It made me hate books and school. It made me disobey my parents for the first time by hiding in woods rather than go to school. School-days were bitter years for me.'

Many Welsh-speaking children suffered in the same way. They were not allowed to speak their own language in school. Schoolmasters and even parents believed that only children who could speak English could hope to get good jobs. Children who found English difficult, and those who just forgot and spoke Welsh, were ordered to wear the 'Welsh Not' or the 'Welsh Stick'. The Welsh Not was a small block of wood with the letters W.N. carved on it. If a child spoke Welsh the block was hung around his or her neck. If that boy or girl then caught another child speaking Welsh, the Welsh Not would be passed on to that child. At

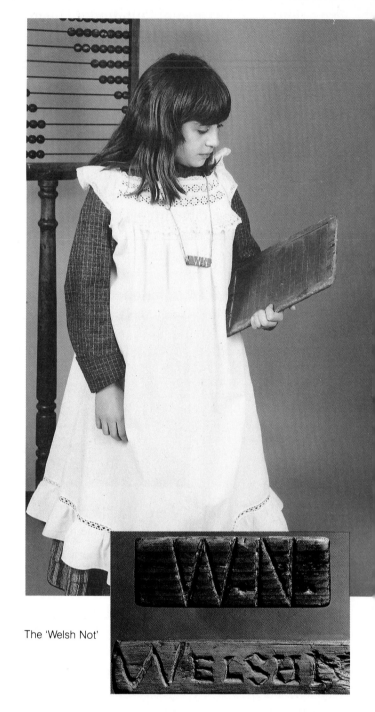

The 'Welsh Not'

the end of the morning the teacher would ask 'Who has the Welsh Not?' The culprit was then severely caned on the hand. Others who had worn the Welsh Not that morning were also caned. Children lived in fear of the cane and were afraid to speak their own language. Even in the most Welsh-speaking areas children were forced to use English spelling-books and learn English poetry. Often they didn't understand the words but recited them like parrots.

The results were hilarious. Children at Talsarnau in North Wales were instructed to sing the popular hymn:

'Let us with a gladsome mind,
Praise the Lord for he is kind.'

But the words which the Welsh children sang were:

'Lettus gwyddau glas a maidd
Pres y lord ffor hyn Rhys cain.'

They thought that the word 'Lord' referred to Lord Harlech who lived nearby!

Welsh children were never taught about Welsh heroes like Llywelyn the Last or Owain Glyndŵr. Only the history of English heroes was taught. When Richard Jones Owen, a poet known as Glaslyn, was a boy he wrote this about his English spelling-book:

'There was one page which contained pictures of people of different nations, such as the English, the Welsh, and the Scots. The Englishman and the Welshman were placed alongside each other. The Englishman was as noble as a prince. But the Welshman by his side was a puny little dwarf.'

Owen Morgan Edwards grew up to be a fine scholar and in 1889 he was appointed history tutor at Lincoln College, Oxford. But he never forgot his miserable school-days. Owen decided to tell Welsh children about their history. In January 1892 he published the first edition of *Cymru'r Plant* (*The Children's Wales*), a popular magazine which cost only a penny. It was brimming with information, games and competitions. Welsh children could read about flowers, trees, birds, music, poetry, painting, cricket and football in their own language. Owen's aim was to 'raise up his native land' by teaching children to appreciate the beauty and history of their country. All his spare time was spent in writing. He never took a holiday and, in all, he wrote or edited ninety books and seven journals.

Two title pages from Cymru'r Plant – The Children's Wales

In 1907 Owen Edwards was appointed Chief Inspector of schools in Wales. 'Little Wales must have better education,' he said. He visited hundreds of schools. He inspired many teachers to use the Welsh language in their teaching. He also ordered them to be kinder to their pupils. Children adored him because he told them so many fascinating stories about history in their own areas. One day he told the children of Monmouth a story about a prisoner in the town's castle. Before he could finish the story he was called away by the headmaster. Then the dinner bell rang. When the headmaster returned to the class in the afternoon the children were still sitting at their desks. Not one of them had gone for lunch. They were all waiting patiently for the Inspector to finish his story.

Owen Morgan Edwards

Urdd Gobaith Cymru

'What shall we, the children of Wales, do, we who live in little Wales, our own country? We must do something because we are the hope of our country. What if we were to unite together to decide that we will do everything that can help our nation?'

This letter appeared in *Cymru'r Plant* in January 1922. It was written by Ifan ab Owen Edwards, the son of Owen Morgan Edwards. Two years earlier Ifan's father had died. Now it was his turn to help young Welsh children. Ifan was brimming with ideas and said he was ready to work day and night 'for the sake of Wales'. Soon after the letter was published, he began his most exciting project – *Urdd Gobaith Cymru*, The Welsh League of Youth.

Ifan's main aim was to protect and foster the Welsh language. He wanted young people to love their country and their culture. He also wanted them to enjoy themselves. 'Lots of fun and lots of Welsh – that's the goal!' he said. By the end of 1922, some 720 children had joined the movement. Each member was given a certificate and a badge. Colourful banners were designed and members promised to be loyal to Wales, their fellow-man, and to Christ. In 1929 the first *Urdd* National Eisteddfod was held at Corwen. Thousands of young people began to join. By 1931, nearly 30,000 had enrolled as members of the *Urdd*. There were branches in towns and villages all over Wales.

There were all kinds of indoor and outdoor activities. Singing, folk-dancing, athletics, football, rugby, craftwork and first-aid were just some of them. Special emphasis was placed on walking, camping, swimming and gymnastics. In 1932 an athletics meeting was held at Llanelli. A crowd of 8,000 enjoyed a splendid gymnastic display performed to the accompaniment of several brass bands.

Permanent holiday camps for teenagers were set up at Glan-llyn, near Bala, and Llangrannog. The *Urdd* 'yell' soon echoed loudly throughout Wales:

'Who are we? Who are we?
Girls of Wales, Boys of Wales,
Welshmen of the country,
    Welshmen of the town,
Welshmen from everywhere
    under the sun,
G - W - A - L - I - A!
GWALIA!'

The *Urdd* badge is seen behind the actors

Above: An *Urdd* pageant

Right: Ifan ab Owen Edwards

By offering something for everyone, the *Urdd* flourished.

As a Christian movement, the *Urdd* also worked for peace and goodwill among all people. Loving and helping other countries was just as important as loving and helping Wales. Every year since 1925 members of the *Urdd* have sent a 'Goodwill Message' to the children of the world. Young people went on cruises to Norway, Spain and the Mediterranean, and set up links with people of their own age in other countries. Ifan ab Owen Edwards encouraged every member to pro-

mote the cause of international peace. 'There is so much to be done,' he used to say, 'and life is so short.' He inspired thousands of people to give freely of their time and money to help the *Urdd*. All of them were proud to be Welsh.

Urdd Gobaith Cymru is still flourishing today. It has over 1,200 branches in Wales. Over a million pounds a year are needed to run the organization. A lot of money is raised by voluntary efforts. The *Urdd* Eisteddfod has continued to grow in popularity. Over 45,000 young people compete to try to reach its final stage. There are all sorts of competitions, ranging from recitation to disco dancing, and folk-singing to swimming. There are also children's pageants and rock operas.

The two holiday centres are also thriving. At Llangrannog and Glan-llyn fluent Welsh-speakers and Welsh-learners ride, roller-skate, row, sail and climb to their hearts' content. Ifan ab Owen Edwards was right: 'Lots of fun and lots of Welsh'. That's the secret behind the success of the *Urdd*.

Burning the Bombing-School

At half-past one at night on 8 September, 1936 three Welshmen crept under a fence surrounding the site of the R.A.F. bombing-school on the Llŷn Peninsula. They carried torches, petrol and matches. They knew that the caretaker of the building site had gone hunting with his dog. Even so, they checked to make sure that nobody would be placed in any danger. The coast was clear! They poured petrol over an empty wooden hut and some building materials. Although their matches were a little damp, they soon managed to start a fire. Within minutes the whole camp was in flames.

The three men didn't run away. They strolled back to their car and drove to the police station at Pwllheli to give themselves up. They told the police that they had burnt down the bombing-school at Penyberth. The three fire-raisers were not cowards or vandals. They were very respectable men. Saunders Lewis was a famous scholar, Lewis Valentine was a minister, and D. J. Williams was a schoolmaster. They were all well-known Welsh writers. Why did they burn down a bombing-school?

Early in 1936 the government decided to build a training site for R.A.F. pilots. They said that the ideal place was Penyberth, a farm in the Llŷn Peninsula. But people all over Wales were outraged. A huge protest movement was launched. Poets, authors, and pacifists wrote angry letters to newspapers. They said that Llŷn had always been a stronghold of Welsh language and culture. Others stressed that

Llŷn was a beautiful part of Wales. A bombing-school would ruin the landscape. Religious people said that pilgrims travelled to the sacred island of Bardsey through Llŷn. The protests grew louder and louder.

Welsh people were even angrier when they found out that the original plan had been to build the bombing-school in England. The first choice was Holy Island in Northumberland. But nature-lovers said it was the home of the shelduck. So the government changed its mind. The second plan was to build the school at Abbotsbury in Dorset. This time nature-lovers said that breeding swans would suffer. So the government finally decided that the Llŷn Peninsula was the most suitable site.

By August 1936, half a million people in Wales had said they were opposed to the plan. In Llŷn and Eifionydd, a petition was signed by 5,300 people. But there were also supporters of the scheme. Unemployed people wanted work at the aerodrome. They turned up at protest meetings to jeer, heckle, and sing 'Rule Britannia'.

The Welsh tried to take their complaint to Stanley Baldwin, the Prime Minister, but he refused to grant them an interview. All the protests were in vain. The birds, swans, ducks and beaches of England were not to be disturbed. The people of Llŷn didn't seem to matter so much. The three Welsh patriots – Saunders Lewis, Lewis Valentine and D. J. Williams – saw this was unjust. So, on 8 September, 1936, as an act of protest, they burned down the bombing-school.

After giving themselves up, the three men were charged with arson. In October they were brought to trial at Caernarfon Assizes. Huge crowds assembled outside the court-rooms. They sang hymns as they waited for the jury's verdict. In the court, the three Welshmen called on the jury to find them 'not guilty'. They said that their only 'crime' was to defend the Welsh nation. In the end, the jury failed to agree on a verdict. When the crowd outside heard the news they cheered for hours. The three Welshmen were freed and were carried shoulder high through the town.

But the judge had ordered another trial. This time the case was heard at the Old Bailey in London. There were no Welsh people on the jury there. Saunders Lewis, Lewis Valentine and D. J. Williams refused to speak in English in the court. They were found guilty of arson and sent to Wormwood Scrubs prison for nine months. While they were in prison, the bombing-school at Penyberth was rebuilt and opened on 1 March, 1937. But Welsh people didn't forget the protest of the three Welshmen. On their release from prison, they were given a heroes' welcome. 12,000 people had packed into Caernarfon Pavilion. Those who were there said they had never heard 'Men of Harlech' sung with such feeling.

Far left: Still from a BBC film about the bombing-school

Left: The three arsonists: Lewis Valentine, Saunders Lewis, D. J. Williams

The Welsh Language Society

Above: Members of The Welsh Language Society protest

Left: The symbol of the Society

It is 1987. Twenty-five years ago *Cymdeithas yr Iaith Gymraeg* – The Welsh Language Society – was formed. During those years young people have staged sit-downs in law courts. They have daubed paint on English road signs. They have climbed up television masts. Many have gone on hunger strikes, and been sent to prison. All over Wales members of the Society have broken the law and made nuisances of themselves. Let's ask one of the language campaigners why these things have happened.

'All of us are worried about the future of the Welsh language. It's the oldest living language in Europe and it's under threat. Time is short and we must defend it.'

He shows us a graph illustrating how the number of Welsh-speakers has declined this century.

'Look at this. Half the people of Wales spoke Welsh in 1900. By 1981 their numbers had halved. I can think of many reasons why this has happened. Motor cars, buses, railways and motorways have brought Wales much closer to England. Many of our young people have to move out of Wales to look for work. They're replaced by English people who can afford to buy rural farms and cottages. Also, the Welsh countryside is so beautiful that the English like to buy holiday homes here. We're afraid that Wales is up for sale. Only a few English immigrants bother to learn Welsh and their children bring the English language into the schools and playgrounds. Most of the education in Wales in this century has been in English. Do you remember what Idris Davies, a poet from Rhymni, sang?

"I lost my native language
For the one the Saxon spake
By going to school by order
For education's sake."

'Over the years people have got used to hearing English on the radio and television. It's no wonder that many people looked on the Welsh language as a nuisance. No one seemed to care about it.'

'Is that why Cymdeithas yr Iaith Gymraeg *was formed?'* we ask.

'Yes. Young Welsh people decided that Welsh-speakers should have the same rights as English-speakers in Wales. Our aim was to fight for the Welsh language. Mind you, we've always used non-violent methods. We've never harmed other people. But we've made the government and local authorities sit up and take notice of us. We've plastered post offices, police stations, and other public buildings with posters and stickers. English-only road signs have been covered with green paint. We've climbed up television masts at night and broken into holiday homes. We've even staged protests in the Old Bailey in London and in the House of Commons.'

'How did people react to all this?'

'Many ordinary people didn't understand why we were protesting. We've been jeered and jostled. Policemen have bundled us into vans. Newspapers have called us vandals and hooligans. But we say the laws we've broken are unjust laws. And we've always been prepared to be fined or sent to prison. Every protest has been peaceful.'

Whatever people may think of the language protesters, some of their methods seem to have got results. More and more people became concerned about the fate of the Welsh language and other societies were set up to help it survive. There are now bilingual road signs and official forms in post offices and banks. The Welsh television channel – *Sianel Pedwar Cymru* – is established. There are over 500 nursery schools where children can learn Welsh. Bilingual secondary schools are increasing in number. More and more young people enjoy folk, pop, and rock music in the Welsh language.

But much more needs to be done if the Welsh language is to survive. Even in Welsh-speaking areas such as Gwynedd and Dyfed the language is losing ground. Time is running out. The Welsh National Anthem says: 'May the old language continue.'

Do you think Welsh people should learn the Welsh language and be proud of it?

A protest on the Eisteddfod field

Superted

41

The South Wales Coalfield

Map of the South Wales Coalfield

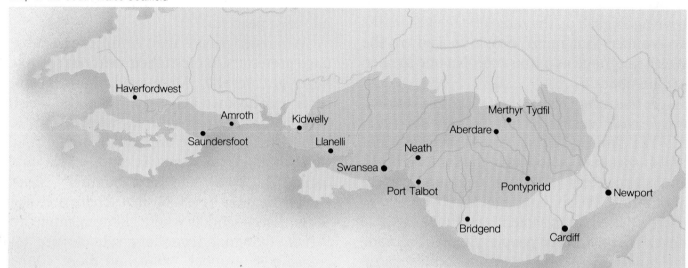

Here is a map of the South Wales Coalfield. You can see that the coalfield is shaped like an oval basin or a crumpled rugby football. It's about 56 miles long and 16 miles wide. In this area thousands of working people produced millions of tons of excellent coal. By 1913 there were 620 coal mines employing 232,000 men and over 17,000 horses. In that same year 57 million tons of coal were produced and most of it was sent, first by rail, and then by steamships, to ports all over the world. Coal made Wales famous.

Horse and tram

You may think that all coal is the same. But coal mined in South Wales varied in thickness and quality from mine to mine and from valley to valley. There were three popular types of coal and each had its uses. The eastern part of the coalfield was the best place to find bituminous coal. This was good house-coal and it was used for fires in open grates in people's homes. It was also used to produce coke and gas. In the Rhondda valleys the finest coal was steam coal. This was 'smoking coal' which always burned brightly and strongly. It was used to power railway engines and steamships. The third type of coal – anthracite coal – was mined in the western part of the coalfield. Anthracite coal produced great heat and was just right for boilers used to heat houses and offices.

Mining coal was a hard and dangerous task. Every miner who went to work underground knew that he was risking his life. Roofs were unsafe, seams were often full of explosive gases, and ventilation was poor. There were no machines to help the miner cut the coal. Pneumatic coal picks were not used in Welsh collieries until the 1920's. So the miner relied on a hand-pick known as a mandril.

Until the 1860's the most popular way of mining coal was the pillar and stall method.

Colliers cut away wedges of coal by working in stalls. Pillars of coal were left behind to support the roof and the roadways. This method was very slow and wasteful. It was also dangerous, especially if colliers were tempted to work coal from the pillars, thereby weakening the roof support.

A better and faster method of mining coal was brought in from the 1860's. This was called the long-wall system. Colliers now worked across the face of the seam in a single line. All the coal was cut away and no pillars were left behind. As the colliers moved forward they used props to support the roof. They filled the space behind them with stone and rubble. Colliers soon found that this method enabled them to work more safely and swiftly.

Pit-head winding gear

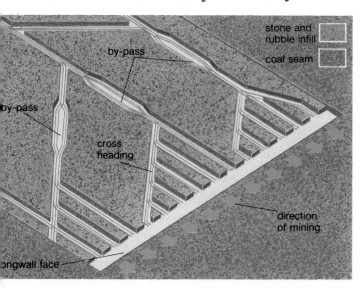

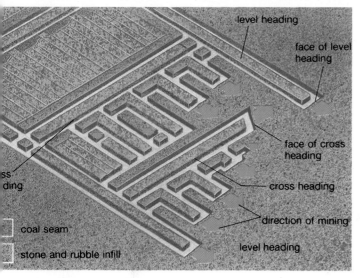

Ways of mining coal

The coal was loaded into trams and pushed by boys to the main roadway. There hauliers hitched the trams to ponies which trotted off to the bottom of the pit shaft. The coal was then hauled to the surface.

As mines got deeper and deeper, the fear of roof falls and explosions increased. Most coalowners wanted quick profits and were not worried about proper safety standards. Mining regulations were issued in English, and many Welsh-speaking workers either couldn't understand them or didn't bother to read them. Some miners preferred using naked lights rather than locked safety lamps, and they paid with their lives for breaking the rules.

There were many injuries and deaths. Miners fell off trams, were crushed to death by roof falls, and were poisoned by gases. In November 1867, 178 men and boys were killed at Ferndale Colliery in Glamorgan. As we shall see later, even worse disasters were to happen.

3

The Gem of Glamorganshire

In 1847 a man called Charles Frederick Cliffe travelled through Glamorgan. This is how he described the upper Rhondda Fawr:

'The Valley stretched for a distance of eight to ten miles between neat parallel lines of hills. The emerald greenness of the meadows of the valley below were most refreshing. The air is aromatic with the wild flowers and mountain plants. A Sabbath stillness reigns.'

Cliffe called the Rhondda Fawr 'the gem of Glamorganshire'. Sheep grazed contentedly in the fields and there were trout and salmon in the streams. The valley was green and very few people lived there.

All this changed when coal was discovered in the Rhondda. From the 1860's onwards thousands of people flocked there. Pits were sunk, roads and railways were built, and villages and towns began to spring up very quickly. By 1913 there were 53 large collieries in the Rhondda, producing $9\frac{1}{2}$ million tons of coal. Steam coal from the Rhondda was known and admired all over the world.

Life in the Rhondda now revolved around

coal. Millions of tons were mined every year and sent in coal trucks by rail to the docks at Cardiff and Barry. Woodland was cleared and mine waste was piled up on the hillsides and moorlands. These mountainous colliery tips looked like the pyramids of Egypt – only they were black!

People came in their thousands to look for work in the Rhondda. Most of them were Welsh people who wanted more money to spend on food and clothes. Wages were higher in the mines than in rural villages, and life seemed more exciting. Therefore, young agricultural workers and farmers left the plough and the reaper for the thriving coal mines of South Wales. Even quarrymen came down

Clydach Vale in the Rhondda

Tylorstown in the Rhondda about 1890

from North Wales. Many took lodgings and once they'd earned enough money to be able to rent a house they sent for their wives and children.

Homes were built as near as possible to the collieries. People lived in long rows of houses which stretched in parallel lines along the hillsides. Houses for working people were built as quickly and as cheaply as possible. As more and more people moved to live in the new industrial villages, terraces began to dominate the hillsides. The number of people living in the Rhondda rose from just over 3,000 in 1861 to 167,000 by 1921. On average, six people lived in each house. After 1880 many labourers from the west of England began to move there too. The English language became common in the Rhondda.

Families took in lodgers in order to help them pay the rent. There were no toilets, bathrooms or piped water. Families shared a privy set over a cess-pit. The barracks built for miners by David Davies, Blaengwawr, were described as 'far too poor for men who work hard in the bowels of the earth.'

There was no clean drinking water, and infectious diseases like diphtheria, dysentery and typhus were common. Seepages from collieries and foul-smelling overflows poisoned local streams, rivers and wells.

In 1893 a government inspector described the Rhondda Fawr like this:

'The rivers contain a large proportion of human excrement, stable and pigsty manure, congealed blood, offal and entrails from the slaughterhouses, the rotten carcasses of animals, cats and dogs in various stages of decomposition, old cast-off articles of clothing and bedding, old boots, bottles, ashes, street refuse and a host of other articles.'

The whole valley had changed dramatically since Charles Frederick Cliffe's journey in 1847. The old pastoral beauty and stillness had been replaced by busy, noisy collieries and over-populated industrial villages.

Davies the Ocean

The growth of the coal industry in South Wales would never have happened without the money and energy and ambition of the coalowners. Rich coalowners provided money to sink pits and offered thousands of men jobs. They were ready to take risks in order to make large profits. One of the best-known coal-owners was David Davies, the son of a Montgomeryshire farmer. Do you remember reading about him in the section on 'The College by the Sea'? As a young man, David Davies was known as 'Top Sawyer' because he was so good at felling trees. Later on he became a successful railway contractor. He was the first to bring the 'iron horse' into mid-Wales. People soon noticed that he had plenty of energy and a flair for getting things done.

Statue of David Davies at Barry Docks

Coal trucks at Maindy colliery

When the 'coal rush' began in South Wales, David Davies seized his chance. In 1864 he and five other wealthy men bought the leases of 2,000 acres of land in the Rhondda Valley. In January 1865 two shafts were sunk at the Parc and Maindy pits, and David Davies and his friends sat back and waited for news. But after fifteen months of hard work his miners still hadn't found any coal. Davies had spent £38,000 by this time and he didn't have any more savings left. He was bitterly disappointed.

One Saturday morning in 1866 David Davies called his miners together to tell them the bad news:

'Well, boys, I'm sorry to tell you that I can't go on here any longer. I'm very sorry because I believe there's some grand coal here and that we're close to it.'

Painting of the entrance to Barry Docks in 1898

After paying them their final wage packets, Davies said, 'That leaves half a crown in my pocket'. One of his men called out, 'We'll have that too.'

'Take it,' said Davies. He tossed him the coin and walked away sadly.

When he had gone his workmen gathered round and began to talk about their future. They argued for some time, but in the end they decided to take a gamble. Because Davies had been such a fair and generous employer, they were ready to work for a whole week without pay. They, too, must have known that deposits of coal weren't far away. They were right! On the following Friday, the ninth of March, they whooped with delight when they found rich deposits of excellent steam coal. David Davies was overjoyed when he learned the news.

From then on thousands of tons of coal were mined and exported, and David Davies became a very rich man. In 1867 he formed the 'David Davies Coal Company'. Later on, the company became known as the Ocean Coal Company Limited. By 1894 the thousands of miners employed by the company were producing two million tons of coal a year. David Davies was known throughout Wales as 'Davies the Ocean'. He was very proud of Welsh coal. On one occasion, when he was invited to give a speech in front of 600 Englishmen, he told them that Welsh coal was the best coal in the world.

In order to export his coal to all parts of the globe David Davies decided to build a new dock at Barry. The work of excavation was done by 3,000 navvies, and the docks took five years to build. When Barry docks were opened in July 1889 the whole venture had cost £2 million. From then on, coal poured into the holds of ships hour after hour, day after day. Shunters, tippers and trimmers worked like beavers and ships' captains always praised Barry because goods were moved so quickly to and from the docks. By 1913 Barry was exporting over eleven million tons of coal a year to countries all over the world.

Not many Welshmen have two statues in their honour. David Davies is one who has. There is a statue of 'Davies the Ocean' in front of the Dock offices in Barry. A copy of the same statue stands in his native village of Llandinam in Montgomeryshire.

The Welsh Miner

Undercutting coal with a mandril

Welsh miners were very strong and brave men. They needed to be because life underground was extremely dangerous. At around 4.30 every morning miners' wives or mothers got up to prepare breakfast and hot water for men returning from the night shift. There were no baths at the pits and miners bathed in hot water in wooden tubs in front of the kitchen fire. They were covered in coal dust and grime, and their wives had to scrub them vigorously to get them clean. The next task was to make sure that food and clothes were ready for the day shift. Food tins (known as tommy boxes), water bottles and tea jacks were filled. Miners wore a flannel shirt, trousers, a leather belt, a muffler around the neck, a cloth cap, a heavy coat, and hob-nailed boots.

As they walked to the pits, the miners chatted and joked. The streets echoed loudly to the sound of their heavy hob-nailed boots. Once they reached the pit-head they got ready to go down into the mine in a cage. It was always a bone-shaking journey. When they reached the bottom they often had to walk as much as a mile to reach their place of work. It was pitch black down the mine. Roofs were low and the passages were narrow. It was cold, wet and miserable. The collier worked in such cramped conditions that he often had to cut coal either on his knees or lying on his side. It wasn't easy to learn how to lie on one's side and still be able to swing one's elbows in order to chip away the coal with a mandril. Black, oily water hampered his task and squealing rats scampered to and fro.

A miner's shift lasted for ten or twelve hours. Not until the Miners' Eight Hour Day Act of 1908 did long working hours end. But for most men there were no jobs except those down the pits. Some miners worked underground for nearly all their lives. David Davies, who was born at Pont-rhyd-y-fen in the Afan valley in 1842, started work at the age of seven in Maerdy in the Rhondda. He didn't retire until he was 80 years of age! In winter, miners like David Davies only saw daylight on Saturdays and Sundays. This is what Gwilym Tilsli, a Welsh poet, wrote in his 'Ode to the Collier':

'The acres of coal under the floor of the glen
– is his place
With his lamp and tool;
To his dark cell bright day comes not,
The sun will not follow him there.'

Miners worked together in teams and they often risked their own lives in order to rescue trapped or injured comrades. The fear of sudden death was with them all the time. At any moment miners might be burnt, drowned, suffocated or crushed. Between 1844 and 1871, 914 men and boys were killed by explosions in the coal mines of Glamorgan. Miners had to learn to get used to the coal and shale dust, and the horrible smell of gas. Many of them suffered from asthma and bronchitis. Thousands died of 'the dust' – a disease of the

Tarian y Gweithiwr.

"Nid Amddiffyn ond Tarian." "Goreu Tarian, Cyfiawnder."

Cofnodydd Helyntion Gweithfaol, Llenyddol, a Gwleidyddol, yn nghyda Newyddion Cymreig, Cyffredinol, a Thramor.

GWENER, GORPHENHAF 7, 1876.

Rhif 78.] [Pris Ceiniog.

Miners at work at Lewis Merthyr

A bath in front of the fire

lung called silicosis. Even today there are retired miners who gasp for air as they climb the stairs or stagger to the shops.

Because of the dangers underground there was always a strong sense of togetherness among miners. Young men and boys were taught the tricks of the trade by older 'butties'. Miners had plenty of jokes and funny stories to tell as they worked in groups. Nearly all of them had nicknames like Ianto Shwmae, Dic Bol Haearn, Billy Welsh Cake and Dai Whiff,

Cough and Spit. They were very superstitious people. If they happened to forget their tommy box they never returned home to fetch it because that was unlucky. Some older miners only washed their backs once a week because they believed that too much hot water weakened the spine and robbed them of their strength. They were always happy to have rats around them in the mines. If the rats vanished, miners knew that some terrible disaster was sure to happen.

Going Down the Pit

It's Morgan's twelfth birthday today. He's hardly slept a wink all night. His big day has arrived at last. He's about to join his father down the pit. Morgan's father had always talked to him about the trams, the pit-horses, the stalls and his butties at work. All kinds of funny stories had made him laugh. But he also remembers the tale of young boys crushed by trams and lying in a pool of blood crying 'Mam, Mam'. He'd noticed the relief on his mother's face when his father returned safely from the pit, his face black with coal dust and the whites of his eyes gleaming. Morgan worshipped his father. He was a strong, muscular man with a long scar on his cheek. He had a fine tenor voice and he was as strong as an ox in the pack of the village rugby team. Morgan had longed for the chance to work alongside him. Now his dream was about to come true. He can tell us about his experiences on his first day down the pit.

'I was nearly too excited to eat my breakfast that morning. My mother had filled my plate with eggs, bacon and fried bread, and she warned me to eat every bit of it because there was a long day ahead of me. My father agreed. He said that every good miner went to work on a full belly. My mother put my food in a small tin box and filled a tin jack with cold tea. I'll never forget what she said when she opened the front door and kissed me on the cheek:

"May the Lord bring you home safely."

'It was a cold, grey morning, but I hardly noticed the mist and the stiff breeze. I was wrapped up warmly in a thick coat and muffler. Other miners and boys were tramping to work and the sound of hob-nailed boots on the cobbled street was deafening. I was thrilled to reach the pit-head and see the iron trams,

Tip girl at Tredegar   Boy with a lamp

the railway tracks, the machinery and the huge tips of coal and waste. I'd always dreamed of seeing the inside of a pit for myself. I was given a long gauze lamp which my father called a sprag. A hooter blew and I followed my father into the pit-cage. Crushed among a dozen men and boys I closed my eyes and gripped my lamp tightly. Down went the cage. It was like falling through the bottom of the earth. My stomach turned upside down, I gasped with fright, and grabbed my father's arm. It was completely dark.

'I was so relieved to reach the bottom. My father said we'd travelled a quarter of a mile in the cage, but it seemed more like a hundred miles to me. At the pit bottom there were crowds of men, boys and horses. We set off for the coal-face. My father had warned me that we'd have to walk nearly a mile to reach it. We walked along long, narrow tunnels. There were ponds of water everywhere. Water trickled down from the roof and I shivered when it ran down my back. The air was stale and there was a faint smell of gas. Squealing rats frightened the life out of me, but my father just laughed and told me they were my friends.

'I couldn't believe how narrow the space was at the coal-face. My father knelt down to cut the coal with his mandril. I had to fill the tram with the coal he cut. I worked much slower than the others but I was determined to learn the collier's skills and to grow up to be as strong as my father. By the end of the day my whole body ached, and the skin on my hands and knees was raw. When I got home at 5.30 in the afternoon my face and hands, my pit-lamp, box and jack were as black as soot. My father said I'd done well and that I'd got the makings of a miner. His praise was music to my ears. My mother hugged me tightly and then began to fill the empty bath with piping hot water. I'll never forget that first day down the pit!'

Coal Out, Grain Home

As we've seen, thousands of tons of coal were mined in the South Wales Coalfield. Where did it all go? Much of it was carried by rail to the docks at Cardiff. There it rattled down the coal chutes and was transferred into large steam-ships which sailed to all parts of the globe. In 1801 fewer than 2,000 people lived in Cardiff, but a hundred years later it was no longer a small market town. It was a large city of over 182,000 people by 1911. It was not only the biggest city in Wales but also the largest coal-exporting port in the world. In 1886 the Cardiff Exchange was opened. Its offices were the headquarters of the coal trade in South Wales.

Let's visit the docks. We'll talk to John Owen, a seaman on board the S.S. *Bala*, a

tramp steamer built in 1884. He's a stocky man with a friendly, weather-beaten face. He will tell us about his experiences as an able-bodied seaman.

'I used to be a fisherman catching shoals of herring in Cardigan Bay. But I never earned enough to keep my wife and five children. A friend of mine told me about the modern steamers which carried coal from Cardiff to faraway ports. I'd always wanted to sail on wider oceans and see the world, so I took a chance and joined the Messrs. Evan Thomas, Radcliffe Shipping Company. I've never re-gretted it. Come on board!'

We climb on to the deck of S.S. *Bala*. John Owen tells us that the ship was built in West Hartlepool and bought by Captain Evan Thomas, a master mariner, and Henry Rad-cliffe, a shipping clerk.

'She's a solid old ship and I'm quite fond of her. You can see she's made of iron. When the engine gets up a fair head of steam she can just about manage a speed of nine knots. But a lot depends on how much coal we carry. She's got four holds which can store around 2,600 tons of cargo. There are four steam winches for loading coal and other goods. We've carried thousands of tons of coal to the ports of France and Italy. We've even been to some of the ports in the Black Sea like Odessa and Sulina. Once we've dumped the coal into bunkers we bring back cargoes of cereal to Cardiff. We call it the "coal out, grain home run".'

We ask John Owen to tell us about life on board S.S. *Bala*.

'It's no picnic, I can tell you. I work up to ninety hours a week and I only get away to see my family in Llangrannog about once every two or three months. It's hard for them

Painting of the S.S. *Bala*

Entrance to the Bute West Docks

because when I'm away for so long they never know whether I'm alive or dead. But the wages are quite good. I earn up to £3 a month if I'm lucky. But I say that anyone who goes on long ocean passages deserves a decent wage. We had some terrifying moments on our last trip to Odessa. A fierce gale blew up and water began to pour into the holds. A couple of seamen were swept overboard and I thought my number was up. But the storm passed by and we breathed a huge sigh of relief. Mind you, it's pretty awful below deck even when the weather's not too bad. Our bunks are rivetted to the hull of the ship, so it's hard to sleep when the sea's rough. You ought to see the fleas, bugs and cockroaches in my mattress! Our

rations are poor. The meat is always tough, the bread and biscuits stale, and the tea like washing-up water. On most voyages we have sea pie. We call it cracker hash – it's made of layers of salt-meat, ship's biscuits and peas. Ugh! You can't blame us for smuggling a few bottles of spirits on board. With a few drinks inside us we can sing hymns as well as any chapel choir in Wales.'

We thank John Owen and move on to gaze at the fleet of large ships glistening in the sun in Cardiff docks. We note some of their names: S.S. *Llanberis*, S.S. *Glanystwyth*, S.S. *Iolo Morgannwg*, S.S. *Gwenllian Thomas*.

Sometimes these ships changed their names. In 1903 S.S. *Bala* – John Owen's ship – was sold for £8,900 and was re-named S.S. *Glanhowny*. But by this time the ship was getting old and needed lots of repairs. As it happened, on the twenty-fifth of May, 1907, the S.S. *Glanhowny* sank during a journey to Antwerp. Its new owners, however, had insured the ship for £13,500, that is, over £4,500 more than its real worth! Some people claimed that the ship had been sunk deliberately. What do you think?

The Deep and Mighty Waters

On Wednesday the eleventh of April, 1877, miners were hard at work in the Tynewydd Colliery in the Rhondda Valley. Suddenly, water began to pour into the mine from a neighbouring pit. The terrified miners ran for their lives and most of them reached safety. But five miners were trapped. They began to pray and sing and, fortunately for them, a rescue party heard them singing. The rescuers began to hack away the coal. On the following day they heard the trapped miners shouting to them. But as the rescue party broke through, one of the trapped miners, a young man called Thomas Morgan, was hurled by compressed air against the opening. His head became jammed and he died instantly. The other four miners were brought out safely.

That wasn't the end of the story. On Friday more tapping sounds were heard in the mine. No one knew how many men were still alive. Engineers sat down to try to work out how best to rescue the trapped men. Plans of the mine showed that in one direction there were coal deposits 38 yards in length between the trapped men and safety. In another direction there was a huge underground lake. Eventually, the mine's managers decided to try to reach the men by water. They sent for help from London. Two experienced divers – Frank Davies and Thomas Purvis – answered the call and travelled to Tynewydd. They bravely volunteered to venture down into the murky waters in the mine. They wore bell-like helmets, diving suits and heavy lead shoes to keep them stable as they walked down the slope. Tied by rope, they waded into the flooded mine. They went deeper and deeper. But when they reached 500 feet below the surface they were forced to turn back. The current was far too strong for them. The divers were exhausted when they reached the surface. They were very disappointed, but everyone knew they had done their best.

Now the engineers had to think again. Their next plan was to pump water out of the mine. On Saturday and Sunday every available

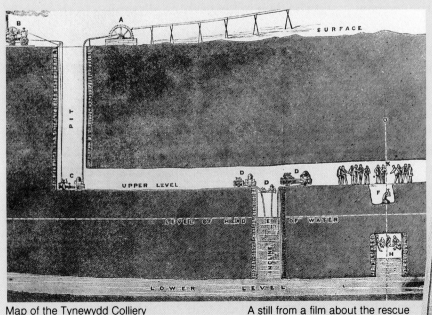

Map of the Tynewydd Colliery

A still from a film about the rescue

A medal which was given to one of the Tynewydd rescuers

pump was used. Locomotives were borrowed from the Taff Vale Railway Company to supply steam to the pumps underground. By Monday morning thousands of gallons of water had been emptied from the mine. The way was now clear for rescue parties to begin cutting through the solid wall of coal. Six groups of four men worked shifts around the clock. They began to cut a hole six feet wide and three feet high. They worked like slaves, raining blow after blow on the black seam.

Early on Wednesday morning the rescuers heard faint cries in the distance. Some miners were still alive! Cheered by the news, they worked even harder. Tapping sounds got closer and soon they could hear muffled shouts of 'hello'.

By this time reporters were filling the newspapers with the story. Every little detail was reported in the London newspapers as well as in the local press. Even Queen Victoria followed reports of the rescue very closely. Hundreds of people gathered at the pit-head waiting for more news. Many of them prayed for the trapped miners.

As the rescuers moved closer towards the trapped men, the work became much more dangerous. The experts warned them that a gas explosion was likely at any moment. They knew, too, that when compressed air was released they could be drowned by flood water. But they struggled on heroically without thinking of the risk to their own lives. On Friday – eleven days after the flooding – the rescuers finally broke through the wall of coal.

They found four men and a twelve-year-old boy. They were still alive. They were perched on a high ledge above the flood water. None of them had eaten for ten days and nights, and they were as weak as kittens. In the darkness they had lost count of the number of days, but they had kept their spirits up by singing the famous Welsh hymn:

'In the deep and mighty waters
None there is to hold my head,
But my dear Saviour Jesus
Who was doomed in my stead.'

No time was lost in lifting the men out of the mine. They were wrapped in blankets and carried on stretchers to safety. For many years afterwards people told the tale of the courage of the rescuers and the rescued in the murky waters of Tynewydd Colliery.

Disaster at Senghennydd

At 4.30 in the morning on the fourteenth of October, 1913, miners in the village of Senghennydd, about ten miles north of Cardiff, were waking up and getting ready to face another long shift. A plateful of eggs, bacon and bread awaited them on the breakfast table. Their wives or mothers were filling their tommy boxes with bread and cheese, and their jacks with cold tea. Soon hundreds of miners were trudging through the dark streets of Senghennydd to the pit. Their pit was the Universal Colliery, owned by Lewis Merthyr Consoli-

dated Collieries Limited. The pit usually produced 500,000 tons of coal every year. But it was a dangerous mine, full of poisonous gases and choking dust. At 5.10 the miners collected their lamps, entered the cages and descended the pit. An hour later there were 950 miners hard at work in two shafts 650 yards below the surface. The two shafts were called the 'Lancaster' and the 'York'.

At 8.10, when mothers were telling their children to finish their breakfast and set off for school, an enormous explosion was heard. One

A young mother waits for news

A funeral at Senghennydd

miner said it was like 'the crack of doom'. Women and children ran from their homes and hurried uphill to the colliery. There was a dark pillar of smoke rising from the mine.

Edward Shaw, the manager of the Universal Colliery, called for the rescue brigades. A huge fire was raging on the west side of the Lancaster shaft. There was so much smoke and heat that rescuers couldn't get near the trapped miners. Even those wearing breathing apparatus were driven back. Red Cross workers, members of the Salvation Army, and ambulance men stood by helplessly. Mothers, wives and children waited in tears at the pithead. Would they ever see their loved-ones again?

That evening a handful of survivors were found and this gave relatives fresh hope. But by the following morning all hope had faded. Hundreds of men had been blasted or burned to death. Stretcher parties carried scores of dead bodies out of the mine. Many of the dead were so badly burned or mutilated it was impossible to tell who they were. Four hundred and thirty-nine miners had died. It was the worst disaster in the history of British coalmining.

Nearly every family in Senghennydd suffered losses. Fathers and sons, brothers and uncles had been killed during the thunderous explosion. Forty-five men who had lived in Commercial Street were dead. Another thirty-five from High Street had died. Every street and every family were in mourning. People wept openly for days. Scores of funerals were held and ministers of religion did their best to comfort the bereaved. Breadwinners had been lost, and so had chapel deacons, choristers, rugby players and fist-fighters. A miner called William Hyatt was lucky enough to escape and never went back to work underground. He said:

'My father always said there was more fuss if a horse was killed underground than if a man was killed. Men came cheap – they had to buy horses!'

An inquiry was held into the disaster in Cardiff in January and February 1914. Over 21,000 questions were asked of witnesses, but no one could tell for certain why the explosion had happened. Some claimed it was caused by exploding gas. Others said that electrical sparks had started the fire. Still others believed that a naked flame kept in the lamp room a quarter of a mile from the bottom of the pit was the real cause of the explosion. In the end, it was decided that safety laws had been broken and that the owners and the manager of the Universal Colliery should be prosecuted. But nothing could bring back the brave miners who had lost their lives on that dreadful autumn morning. Life went on. The Universal Colliery soon replaced the lost miners. Mining was carried on in the pit until it was closed for ever in 1928.

Riot at Tonypandy

Poor safety conditions in coal mines led to injury and death. Miners blamed the coal-owners, claiming that they always placed profit before the safety and welfare of the men. The coalowners had become very rich and power-ful. Some of them treated the miners like slaves. They bought up the small coal com-panies and made them into huge companies called 'combines'. Combines were very un-popular. One miner said: 'the combine is a vast machine, and the worker is merely a cog in it'. Coalowners no longer knew the names of their workers and they refused to pay them a decent wage. Angry miners who worked for the Pow-ell Duffryn Company said that the initials P.D. stood for 'Poverty and Death'. More and more miners joined trade unions in order to protect themselves. But they knew that the coal-owners would punish them and their families if they went on strike or took part in protests and riots.

One of the biggest combines in the South Wales Coalfield was the Cambrian Combine. It was owned by David Alfred Thomas who later became known as Lord Rhondda. He employed 12,000 men who produced over half the coal mined in the Rhondda. In the late summer of 1910 the employers and miners at the Ely Pit in Tonypandy quarrelled over pay. A new seam of coal had been found and because it was so difficult to work miners wanted 2s. 6d. a ton as payment. But the employers were only prepared to pay 1s. 9d. a ton. The two sides couldn't agree. So, on the first of September,

A ransacked shop

A young boy called Bryn Lewis was also watching the riot. This is what he said about the events of that night:

'They started smashing the windows. They smashed this shop here, J. D. Jones, a millinery shop. On the other side here there was Richards the Chemist – they smashed that. And they smashed the windows of these three small shops here; one was a greengrocer, the other one was fancy goods and the other one was a barber's shop ... Oh, there was a huge crowd.'

employers sacked eighty men and locked hundreds of miners out of the Ely Pit. Other miners employed by the Cambrian Combine went on strike. By October there were 12,000 of them. In November 30,000 men were on strike throughout the coalfield.

The striking miners tried to stop the coalowners from bringing in 'blacklegs' – workers from other areas to do their jobs. They also prevented colliery officials from using the pumps which kept the pits from flooding. On Monday, 7 November, a large protest meeting was held outside the Glamorgan Colliery at Llwynypia. Colliers and policemen fought like tigers, stones were thrown, and many people were injured. Captain Lionel Lindsay, chief constable of Glamorgan, was so afraid that he asked the government to send in troops to help him. Winston Churchill, the Home Secretary, promised to send constables from London. Troops were also placed on standby.

The following day thousands of miners gathered outside the Glamorgan Colliery. They clashed with the police. The fighting got worse and strikers poured into the town of Tonypandy. They began to smash shop windows and steal or scatter all sorts of goods. A police constable called Knipe described what he saw:

'It was really hell. We had a terrible job driving them back to the Square. They wrecked all the shops and the whole of the time we could do nothing about it. They drove us back every time.'

Before long the main street was full of top hats, dummies, silks, frocks, cigarettes, vegetables, fruit, sweets and tobacco. The only shop which the rioters refused to touch was a chemist shop owned by Willie Llewellyn. He was a local hero because he had played for Wales against the All Blacks in the famous win in 1905! But the rest of the town centre was a mess. In all, sixty-three shops were damaged.

On 8 November Winston Churchill, the Home Secretary, sent a telegram to General Sir Neil Macready telling him that cavalry should be moved to Tonypandy 'without delay'. Infantry from the West Riding of Yorkshire and Lancashire arrived on 9 November. The 18th Hussars were stationed at Pontypridd.

The strike dragged on for ten months. It caused great hardship and misery. In the end the miners were forced to return to work on 1 September, 1911. They had fought hard to secure a proper living wage and they never forgave Winston Churchill for sending troops to Tonypandy.

Police at the Tonypandy strike

The General Strike

Brynmawr soup kitchen in 1926

Welsh miners believed they had been betrayed by the government. After the First World War ended in 1918, wages were cut and jobs were lost. The Royal Navy began to use oil-fired engines and the demand for coal fell sharply. Coalowners tried to persuade the miners to accept smaller wages and to work an extra hour every day. But the miners' reply was:

'Not a minute on the day. Not a penny off the pay.'

For nine days in May 1926 Britain came to a standstill. Buses and trains stopped running, mines and factories closed down, ships lay idle in the docks. Working people stayed at home. Stanley Baldwin, the Prime Minister, was furious. He said that the General Strike would ruin Britain. But on 12 May the Trade Union Congress called off the strike. Everyone went back to work – except the miners.

The miners refused to give in. They were very angry and bitter. Throughout the fine summer months of 1926 they did their best to help each other. Striking miners weren't given any unemployment pay. Many families were poorer and hungrier than ever before. Sympathetic people set up soup-kitchens to feed the needy. Miners' families were given boiled beef, boiled potatoes, corned beef, soup, bread, cheese, tea and cocoa. Farmers gave vegetables and meat to the very poor. Because so many children walked barefoot to school, co-operative boot centres were set up to repair their boots and shoes.

While the sun shone things weren't too bad. Miners went swimming, played cricket and football, and took part in carnivals. Their children pilfered apples and pears. Some people called it the 'jazz band strike'. Many new jazz bands were formed and these went on tour to entertain strikers and raise money to help their families. Some of these bands were the Cwmparc Gondoliers, the Maerdy Harem Band and the Treorchy Zulus. They were fun to listen to.

But when autumn brought rain and cold weather, it was harder for families to cope. Every day hundreds of miners went out to dig for coal on the mountain tops. Sometimes their children went with them to 'pick the tops'. There were some nasty clashes with the police when miners threw stones at blacklegs. In the end, hunger drove the miners back to work. On 1 December they returned to the pits where they were forced to accept a cut in wages and to work an extra hour each day. Many miners were branded trouble-makers and not taken back by the coalowners.

Those who lived through the seven month strike of 1926 never forgot the suffering and the bravery of the miners. This is what the poet, Idris Davies, wrote:

'Do you remember 1926?
    The great dream and the swift disaster,
The fanatic and the traitor,
    and more than all,
The bravery of the simple, faithful folk?'

A 'jazz band' during the strike

The Slump

The years after the General Strike were miserable ones for working people in South Wales. As the demand for coal fell, collieries were closed down. Many miners lost their jobs. By 1932, 44% of the men in Wales were out of work. In some towns nine out of ten workers had no jobs. The government did very little to help unemployed families. In 1928 an unemployed man received only £1. 3s. 0d. (£1.15) and an extra 2s. (10p) for each child not in work. Many families could barely afford to live on such a pittance. Things got worse in 1931 because a Means Test was brought in. This meant that the head of the family had to disclose every single penny of his earnings and savings. The Means Test caused a great deal of distress and embarrassment. Everybody hated it.

Rhondda miners on a hunger march

The days were long for men without jobs. They spent hours standing in queues waiting for their dole money. Some killed time by working on allotments or repairing broken household items. Others kept racing pigeons or played billiards and snooker in the village hall.

Whenever they could, they took their children to the pits to scramble for unwanted coal. Unemployed men didn't have any spare money to spend in pubs, cafes, shops and cinemas. Many shops and theatres closed, buildings deteriorated and fell down, and piles of rubbish lay in the streets. Everyone was gloomy and downhearted.

Poor families had never known such suffering. The little money they had was used to buy food and to pay rents and small debts. The only shops which did well were the pawn-shops. Many children were pale and thin because there was little nourishing food for them. They had no proper clothes or boots to wear. Many of them suffered from scarlet fever, diphtheria and tuberculosis. Over a thousand men, women and children died of tuberculosis in the Rhondda in 1937. When Edward, Prince of Wales, visited Merthyr and Dowlais in 1936 he was distressed to see so much pain and suffering. 'Something must be done', he said. But little help came.

As we've seen already, Welsh miners were proud men and they protested loudly. Thousands of them took part in hunger marches. They waved banners and chanted 'Down with the Means Test'. Marchers went as far as Bristol and London.

Since there were no jobs for them, young people left the valleys in search of regular work. Between 1921 and 1939, 450,000 people left the Rhondda. They found work and settled in places as far afield as Birmingham, Coventry, Dagenham and London.

Things didn't improve much until the Second World War ended in 1945. Aneurin Bevan, a man born in Tredegar, became Minister of Health. Bevan was the son of a miner and had seen much unnecessary suffering among poor mining families. He believed that the rich and the poor should be given the same standards of health care.

Aneurin Bevan

From 1948 onwards, every family had the right to have free treatment from doctors, dentists and opticians. Weekly payments were given to the sick and the unemployed. Pensions were given to men over 65 and women over 60. Family allowances meant that children could wear decent clothes and shoes. The work that Aneurin Bevan started in London did much to lessen the hardships that the people of South Wales had suffered in the 'Hungry Thirties'.

Women Against Pit Closures

Women protest against pit closures

It is February 1985. We have come to talk to the wives of Welsh miners at Maerdy in the Rhondda. The miners of South Wales have been on strike since 5 March, 1984, and their wives are doing all they can to support them. As we enter the hall where miners' families are being fed, cries of 'Here we go, here we go!' ring out. The wives then chant:

'We are Maerdy miners' wives
Standing at our husbands' sides,
Fighting for the right to work,
Unity is strength.'

To find out why the miners are on strike we will talk to Mrs. Weaver, a miner's wife.

'We're a hundred per cent behind our men. We're determined to protect jobs, pits and communities in South Wales. The government wants to close pits because it puts profit before people. But we're not going to let the Valleys die. There are already hundreds of young men on the dole around here. If the pits close, where will miners find jobs? We think Welsh coal has a future. What's the point of importing coal from Poland or South Africa when we've got the best coal in the world right here? The Coal Board tells us there are geological problems, but we all know that most of our pits have got years of working life left in them. If this pit closes, my sons will have to join the dole queues or move to live in England. Why should they be forced to do that? This is where our roots are. My father and grandfather worked in this pit. We're happy here and we have a right

Vanishing Pit Jobs

E SMITH,
al Editor

eology and
policies — the
uth Wales col-
r the past
now threaten
the coalfield.

leak assessment
es miners' presi-
itfield after yes-
sures and the
s soon to be an-
Bells Colliery,

aid that as long
l continues to
financial com-
e fate of every
liery hangs in the

aid, "These latest
tainly in keeping
board's policy of
lly competitive,
's geology poses
possibility, even
oal is of high

aid British Coal's
t anyone who
in in the industry
nsferred, simply
other pits would
make room.

a tragedy this is
an area that al-
rom high unem-
ng men are losing
he collieries, and
have already left.
they have of fin-

Year	Number
1984	21,500
1985	19,700
1986	16,700
1987	10,200
1988	8,000
1989	6,000

Year	Number
1948	113,000
1958	100,000
1968	45,000
1978	29,000
1988	8,000

GRAPHICS: DES PRICE

"It is irrespon
Coal to shut the
ployment is so hi
she said.
She also warn
plications for
works which th
plied.
The two pit clo
latest round of
lentless blood-
Welsh coal indu
the past 40 yea
Since natior
miners believed
new approach a
wards the indus
of South Wales c
len from more t
ing 113,000 m
employing abou
The pace ha
creased drama
end of the 1984
Nearly 20,000
back into the 28 t
lieries at the end
Most of those p
closed and when
dundacies are im
workforce will ha
nearly two-thirds
The closure of
lights the crisis
more than Lady
the West Glamo
ces anthracite
practically uniq
Wales in Western
that commands a
Such are the
lems of the co
competition from
ducers, that e
collieries are hav
Meanwhile, Bri

acted hastily over closure of
Lady Windsor-Abercynon Colliery

and merged with Lady Windsor
to give it a long life."

to expect proper jobs and a decent wage.'

'Tell us what you've been doing to help the strikers.'

'The strike has brought all the women here together and made them want to fight back. It's very hard to keep our men and children properly fed, but we've had lots of support from people in Wales and elsewhere. We've prepared thousands of meals in this hall. We've packed food parcels, organized jumble sales and held sponsored walks and raffles. But that's not all. We've arranged meetings and rallies for mothers and wives who need help. We're fighting for our lives, so you won't see us at home just making beds and washing dishes. It's a tremendous feeling to see thousands of miners' wives marching under the banner "Women Against Pit Closures". I never thought I'd see the day when I'd be making speeches on platforms!'

'Aren't you afraid of getting hurt?'

'Yes, especially after seeing the way in which some of our men have been injured in fights with the police. But we're ready to stand with our men on the picket lines even if we have to go to jail. Every family in this valley is in this together. If we don't keep the pits open our communities will crumble and the only place where you'll see signs of coal mining will be in an industrial museum.'

Mrs. Weaver shows us a verse which a miner's daughter has written:

'My daddy is a miner
I'm proud to say,
But lately it's hard
Without any pay.
Can't buy any clothes
Can't have a new bike,
We barely manage for food
Because of the long strike.
But I'm prepared to wait
For my daddy is right,
No matter how long it takes
We'll put up a good fight.'

The Welsh miners and their families did put up a good fight. The strike lasted for a year. But on 5 March, 1985, the miners proudly marched back to work behind their banners. Since the strike ended, many pits have been closed down and thousands of miners have lost their jobs. In 1948 there were 113,000 miners in Wales. By 1988 their numbers had fallen to 8,000. 'King Coal' no longer reigns in Wales. There are no working pits left in the Rhondda Valley.

The miners march back to work – 5th March 1985

How the People Lived

Betsi Cadwaladr

An engraving of
Betsi Cadwaladr

Until 1914 most working women were poorly treated. Those who worked on farms or in the homes of wealthy people were badly paid. They were expected to obey their masters, work hard, and never grumble. They didn't have the right to vote in elections and few of them had any contact with the outside world. A few women, however, were determined to better themselves. One of them was Betsi Cadwaladr, a young servant-girl from Merioneth.

Betsi was born on a small farm called Penrhiw, near Bala, in 1789. She was one of sixteen children. When she was nine she became a servant in her father's landlord's house. There she was taught to cook, bake, wash, iron and sew. She also learnt to read, write and speak English. But her ambition was to see the world. When she was fourteen she decided to run away. One night she packed her

clothes into a bundle, jumped out of her bedroom window, and walked all the way to her aunt's house in Chester. She felt free at last!

In 1815 Betsi travelled to Europe. She now called herself Elizabeth Davies, a name which she thought was easier for English-speaking people to pronounce. Elizabeth saw many memorable sights during her journeys around the world. She saw dead bodies strewn over the famous battlefield at Waterloo. When she visited slave plantations in the West Indies

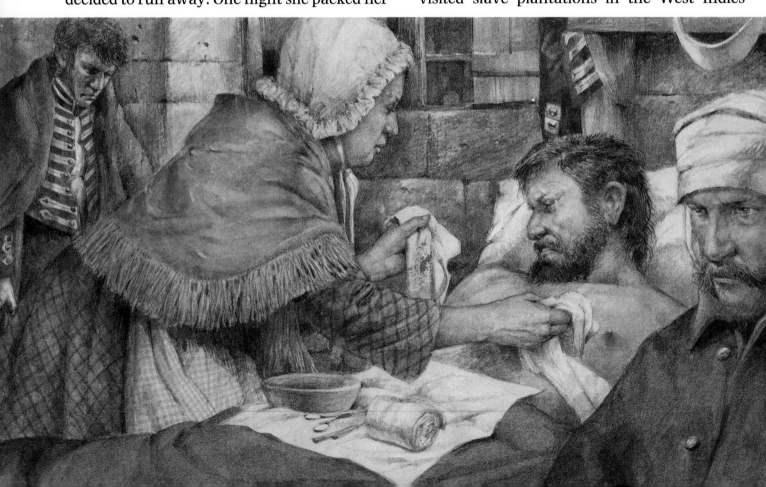

Balaclava harbour and the town

people stared at her and cried, 'What a beautiful foreigner!' She saw rattlesnakes in Chile, a rhinoceros in Africa, and a crocodile in Bengal. On one occasion she saw a fight between a crocodile and a bear!

Eventually Elizabeth decided to be a nurse and she settled down in London. In 1854, when she was 65 years old, Britain went to war against Russia in the Crimea. The war was a disaster. Poorly-led soldiers were outnumbered in battle and many of them died in agony.

There was little warm clothing or food for them, and many wounded soldiers died because of inadequate medical attention. No one knew how awful conditions were until William Howard Russell, a newspaper reporter, sent accounts of the war to Britain. People were outraged. Florence Nightingale and forty other nurses were sent to the Crimea.

When Elizabeth Davies read in the newspapers about the plight of cold, sick and hungry soldiers in the Crimea she decided she must go and help. Florence Nightingale ordered Elizabeth to go to the barrack-hospital at Scutari where she was told to mend old shirts. This made her very angry. She had come to the Crimea to tend the sick. She quarrelled bitterly with Florence Nightingale and said to her: 'Do you think I am a dog or an animal? I have a will of my own.'

Elizabeth was a determined woman and she moved on, without permission, to the hospital at Balaclava. When she arrived she was horrified to find that there were only two surgeons looking after nearly 400 patients. Wounded soldiers were lying on the floors. When she touched a man suffering from frostbite the toes of both his feet fell off. Elizabeth immediately ordered beds for wounded soldiers and then began to clean wounds, apply fresh poultices, and change dressings. Every day she worked from six in the morning until eleven at night. After six weeks she was put in charge of the kitchen. She was a wonderful cook and all the soldiers praised her wholesome food. Many of them called her 'Mother'.

Elizabeth worked so hard that her own health began to suffer and she had to return to Britain. This kind, hard-working and brave woman died in poverty in London in 1860. But we remember her as 'the Welsh Lady with the Lamp'.

How do we know so much about Elizabeth? Very few women, especially if they were poor, left records of their daily lives, thoughts and dreams. But Elizabeth Davies gave a number of interviews to Jane Williams, a scholar and a writer from Ysgafell in Montgomeryshire.

Jane Williams had no tape recorder or typewriter, and so she had to copy down as much as she could remember. We're glad that she did because her tale was well worth telling. But how much, you may wonder, of Elizabeth's story was true?

4

Going to School

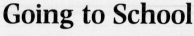

Above: Modern children pose in Victorian costume outside their school

Left: A dame school in Roath village

In the middle of the nineteenth century many poor children never went to school. They were sent out to work on farms, in mines, or in ironworks. But from 1870 onwards more schools were built in Wales, and ten years later education became compulsory for all children. We can tell what life was like in schools in those days by reading the log-books kept by head teachers. And some people have written down what they remember about their early school-days.

Children walked to school. One old lady who, as a child, used to walk to Dunvant School in Swansea said:

'I wore naily boots, which went with our flannel frocks and white pinafores made by our mothers. As we went along the road we had to jump up on the hedge to let the carter and horse go by on his way to Swansea.'

Girls wore long, dark cotton dresses, white lace-trimmed pinafores, long black woollen stockings, and stout boots. Boys wore thick jackets, white collars, and trousers which were buttoned below the knee. They carried small packs of food which their mothers had prepared for them.

Pupils sat in wooden desks which had iron frames and tip-up seats. A roaring fire or stove kept them warm. They practised writing and arithmetic with either chalk and slates or ink and copy-books. Special emphasis was placed on learning to read English. The headmaster of Bethel school, near Caernarfon, wrote in his log-book in August 1880:

'It is disheartening to find that in spite of all our efforts the children continue to be very Welshy in their talk.'

Inspectors used to visit the schools to see how well pupils were developing. Certificates and medals were given to the best pupils on Prize Day.

No school had a gymnasium or a playing field. Teachers often drilled pupils in class by instructing them to stand up straight and stretch their arms and legs. After school examinations pupils were treated to tea parties, picnics and firework displays. Sometimes they were taken on trips to the seaside, to the local fair, or a visiting circus.

Headmasters and teachers were very strict. Mischievous pupils were boxed around the ears or severely caned. Pupils who were late arriving in the morning at Dunvant were lined up in a row by the headmaster. One by one

Drills at Dowlais school

they were cracked across each hand with the cane. And just for good measure they were given another blow across the back of the hand 'until the dust was flying'. Some pupils were so difficult to control that they were expelled from school. In January 1908 the headmaster of Bethel school noted in his log-book:

'Had occasion this afternoon to punish William for disobedience. He told his teacher that his mother had instructed him to go home rather than come to me for punishment. He had also said that his father said he would thrash whatever teacher would touch him. He will probably have to leave for another school.'

When children caught infectious diseases like measles, diphtheria and scarlet fever, schools were closed. Truancy was always a problem. Parents kept children at home to pick stones, shear sheep, whitewash walls, and carry bales of hay at harvest-time. Pupils regularly stayed away from Bethel school on Mondays:

'We had but very meagre attendance today (12 December, 1881), as is generally the case on the Monday following the pay-day. Several children going to Caernarfon on errands, others looking after the houses for the mothers to go.'

The headmaster of Butetown school in Cardiff was at his wit's end by June 1890:

'We have followed the usual routine during the week. Results are not encouraging – the attendance has been so poor again. Truanting appears to have a firm hold upon some boys, and the attendance officer is apparently powerless.'

Life at school was strict and lessons were usually boring and repetitive. Children, therefore, stayed away in large numbers and played football, hopscotch and hide-and-seek in the fields and streets. But when they were caught they were severely beaten with a cane.

The Sunday Schools

How many verses in the Bible can you recite from memory? One? Five? Ten? None? If you had been a member of a Welsh Sunday School in the Victorian period you would have learnt hundreds of verses. In 1884, 10,000 members of Sunday Schools in Llŷn and Eifionydd in Caernarfonshire learnt a total of 2,181,410 verses in a single year! Elsewhere in Wales, young boys and girls in Sunday Schools learnt lengthy portions of the Bible by heart. Levy Lewis, a young boy who worked on the wharves, could recite 35 psalms. David Hughes, a collier's son, memorized 26 chapters of the Old Testament. Rich members of Welsh chapels used to offer prizes such as large bibles or hymn-books to those children who knew most verses. Many sat examinations and were given prizes and certificates.

Sunday Schools were very popular with both children and adults. In 1901 more than a third of the people who lived in the Rhondda were members of Sunday Schools. Schools were held on Sunday afternoons and usually lasted for an hour. They were often divided into infant, junior, senior and adult units. Members were taught to read, to speak clearly, and to think for themselves.

One of the most popular primers used by children was *Rhodd Mam (Mother's Gift)*. Written by John Parry, and first published in 1811, it was a bestseller. Thousands of children could recite every word in *Mother's Gift*. This is what was expected of members of Gorffwysfa Sunday School in Llanberis, Caernarfonshire:

Standard 1: Learn the alphabet, the Lord's Prayer, and chapters 1–7 of *Mother's Gift*.

Standard 2: Learn to read and spell words

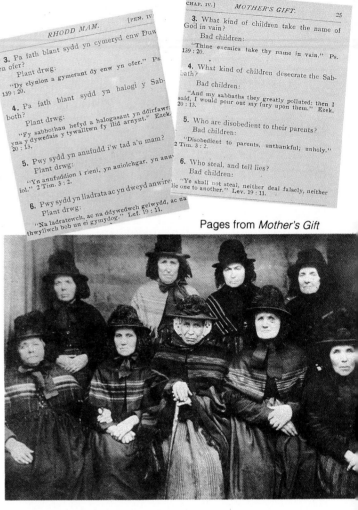

Pages from *Mother's Gift*

Old ladies at Sunday School

of two syllables, and learn *Mother's Gift* from chapter 8 to the end.

Standard 3: Learn to read and spell words of three syllables, and learn the Ten Commandments by heart.
Answer questions on the first twelve years of the life of Jesus.

Mother's Gift contained a series of questions and answers like these:

'Do bad children play on Sundays?
They do.
Do bad children refuse to learn their books in Sunday School?   They do.
Where do bad children go when they die? To hell.'

No wonder children behaved themselves and learnt to recite long passages from the

Bible! They were taught never to break the Sabbath, tell lies, swear, or touch alcohol. Most members of Sunday Schools also went to the Band of Hope during the week. There they promised to be sober and to wage war on 'King Alcohol'. Their teachers warned them of the dangers of strong drink by singing tearful songs about orphans crying for their drunken fathers. This song was very popular among children:

'We are Temperance children,
Dwelling midst the hills,
Working for our Master,

Doing all he wills.
To make the people sober
Is our one great aim,
We are always anxious,
Drunkards to reclaim.'

Children were also encouraged to take part in concerts, eisteddfodau and singing festivals. Penny readings were held in chapel vestries. For a penny, children and adults were able to take part in, or listen to solos, duets and short dramas and sketches. Those children who behaved themselves were rewarded with a trip by train or charabanc to the seaside. The chance to bathe in the sea, ride a donkey, and play football on the sands made learning all those verses worthwhile!

Even as late as 1930, nearly 600,000 children and adults belonged to Sunday Schools in Wales. The oldest among them had been members for over eighty years. Think of how many verses from the Bible you could learn over a period of eighty years!

Left: Two pages from *Trysorfa Y Plant* (*The Childrens' Treasury*), a monthly religious magazine

Below: A Sunday School group in fancy dress

A Little Boy from Merthyr

Joseph Parry's birth place

In 1953 Dylan Thomas, one of Wales's most famous poets, finished his best-known work, *Under Milk Wood*. One of the characters in the play, the Rev. Eli Jenkins, says:

'Praise the Lord! We are a musical nation.'

He was right. Music has always been popular among Welsh people, but especially in the nineteenth century. One man in particular helped the Welsh to learn to love music. His name was Joseph Parry.

Joseph Parry was born in Merthyr Tydfil on 21 May, 1841. His parents were called Daniel and Elizabeth. Joseph's father worked as a refiner in the huge Cyfarthfa ironworks near their home in Chapel Row, Georgetown. At the age of nine Joseph began work down the pits, earning 5d. a day for working a shift of twelve hours. When he was twelve he moved to work with his father in the Cyfarthfa ironworks. Life was hard for young children who were brought up in narrow streets and alleyways and who worked long hours at the dangerous furnaces. At night, when the great furnaces at Cyfarthfa were opened, Joseph must often have gazed upwards and seen the blazing red sky. It looked like a huge volcano erupting.

Joseph's mother was very musical and she taught him many melodies. He sang alto in the Bethesda chapel choir. Close to his home the Cyfarthfa brass band, founded by Robert Thompson Crawshay in 1844, used to practise in the 'Lamb and Flag' tavern. Joseph spent hours listening to the bugles, flutes, French horns, piccolos, trombones and trumpets practising. The sound of music was everywhere in Merthyr. Fiddlers, harpists, minstrels and ballad-singers roamed the streets. Many of them had been badly injured in the mines and ironworks and were now blind or crippled. One newspaper reporter said:

'It is a frequent practice of men disabled to learn to play the harp. They earn a precarious and scanty subsistence by playing at public houses and merrymaking wherever they can find employment.'

Some did quite well. Richard Williams (*Dic Dywyll*), a blind ballad-singer, earned £3 a week singing ballads and folk-songs to the crowds in the streets of Merthyr. He often used to shout 'Penny' in the middle of a word, spit, take the penny, and then carry on singing with hardly a pause!

Joseph's father earned such poor wages that he decided to emigrate to America. In 1854 the rest of the family joined him and settled down to live in Dannville, Pennsylvania. At that time although Joseph had a good singing voice he couldn't read a note of music. But when he was seventeen he was taught to read music by John Abel Jones, a native of Merthyr who worked alongside Joseph in the steel-mills of Pennsylvania. Many young rolling-mill workers, including Joseph, flocked to his music classes after work on Saturday afternoon. Soon Joseph Parry had fallen in love with music. He said:

'From now on. I'm a willing slave to music. I regularly draw on Mr. Jones's wide knowledge. My friends swear that he often says "The little devil, Parry, gives me no peace."'

So he began to compose his own music and compete in eisteddfodau in America and Wales.

In 1865 Joseph returned to Wales to attend the National Eisteddfod at Aberystwyth. He met some of Wales's best musicians – Ieuan Gwyllt, Pencerdd Gwalia, and Ambrose Lloyd – and they liked his work.

He was made a member of the Gorsedd circle and given the bardic name 'Pencerdd America' – America's Chief Poet. His friends in Wales raised enough money to allow him to study at the Royal College of Music in London. There he made a name for himself as a singer and a composer. In 1873 he was appointed Professor of Music at the University College in Aberystwyth. The students adored him and sang happily in his College choir.

Joseph composed music very quickly. One newspaper called him 'the lightning composer'. He did his best to compose a new hymn-tune every Sunday. The Rev. Thomas Levi, who knew him well, spoke of his wonderful memory:

'He's continually composing – in his bed, in a corner, on the road, and in trains. There's no danger of him forgetting one sentence or note.'

Many of Joseph's hymn-tunes, songs, anthems, choruses and operas are still much-loved favourites in Wales. His most popular opera was *Blodwen*, which he completed in 1878. By 1896 it had been performed 500 times. Joseph's hymn-tune, *Aberystwyth*, is one of the finest ever written. And many of you will know *Myfanwy*, one of his most popular songs.

When Dr. Joseph Parry died in February 1903 he was known all over Wales as 'the Great Doctor'. During his burial service at Penarth, over 7,000 mourners thanked him for his efforts on behalf of music in Wales by singing the hymn-tune *Aberystwyth*. Some claimed at the time that he was the best-known Welshman in the world. But up to the day he died Joseph Parry never forgot his roots. In his own words, he was 'a little boy from Merthyr', and always would be.

Cyfarthfa band in 1905

Joseph Parry

Caradog's Choir

A page from the tonic sol-fa

By the 1850's Wales was known as 'the Land of Song'. Printing presses in Welsh towns produced thousands of melodies and song sheets. Shops sold pianos, violins, organs and harmoniums. Large choirs competed against each other in singing festivals and eisteddfodau. They sang the works of some of the most famous composers in the world. Special favourites were *Messiah* by Handel, and *Elijah* by Mendelssohn. But how did children and adults learn to sing? By learning to use the popular and successful method called tonic sol-fa.

Tonic sol-fa was a cheap, accurate and swift way of teaching music in Sunday Schools and choral societies. It was devised by an Englishman called John Curwen. In 1861 a Welsh tonic sol-fa handbook was published. Two years later Ieuan Gwyllt brought out his *Llyfr Tonau* – a collection of hymn-tunes – in sol-fa. Sol-fa classes were set up throughout Wales. Many teachers were chapel ministers or deacons.

Over a period of six months classes of children and adults were taught to sing in tune. Teachers used a tuning-fork, a modulator and a blackboard. A modulator was a chart used in teaching sight-singing. Boys and girls sat in the front, women behind them, and men at the back. They were ordered to sit up straight and keep their shoulders back. Woe betide those who didn't open their mouths or use their lungs properly!

Pupils were instructed to repeat notes after the teacher:

doh   me   soh   doh

They did this first in one key and then in another. Then they were taught notes in more detail:

doh   ray   me   fah   soh   lah   te   doh

These notes form an octave on a keyboard.

Sometimes, instead of using the modulator, teachers used special hand-signals. After many hours of practice these exercises became as natural as breathing to the pupils. They learnt to sing in harmony. Four parts were learnt – soprano, alto, tenor and bass. This helped to make hymn-singing more tuneful and pleasant. Once people understood the tonic sol-fa method they were able to join choral societies and learn the works of composers like Haydn, Handel and Verdi.

Choirs got larger and larger. Some were male voice choirs, others were mixed choirs. Music was very important to working people. They were ready to make long train journeys to attend choir practices. One of the best choirs was *Y Côr Mawr* (The Large Choir), founded by a blacksmith from Abercynon. His real name was Griffith Rhys Jones, but everyone called him 'Caradog'. He was a marvellous conductor. Singers came from as far afield as Llanelli, Neath, Merthyr and Pontypridd to rehearsals at Aberdare. Most of them had learned to sing using the tonic sol-fa method. Caradog was determined to prove that his choir could sing better than any other choir in Britain.

Caradog's big chance came in July 1873. He entered his choir for the famous Challenge Trophy at Crystal Palace in London. By this time there were 457 singers in his choir. Before they left, by train, for London, a final rehearsal was held in Caerphilly Castle. 20,000 people came to listen and to wish them well. When they arrived in London, the organizer of the competition, Willert Beale, said:

'Some of them could not speak English, and many had never before left their native hills – a strange crowd of amateurs, brought together by honest love of music.'

Caradog's choir was up against a very good professional choir from London called the Tonic Sol-fa Association Choir.

Caradog had chosen music by Bach, Beethoven and Mendelssohn, and his choir didn't let him down. They sang splendidly and when they were announced the winners everyone cheered loudly. This is how Willert Beale described the scene:

'The cheering was deafening. The audience, the singers, as well as the friendly opponents of the Welsh choir, joined in the thunderous rejoicing. In every direction hats and caps were thrown in the air. Handkerchiefs, scarves, streamers of ribbon were waved about in the wildest manner. Hands were grasped, embraces exchanged. Men and women were seen to shed tears in the ecstasy of their delight. The Welsh choir had won!'

When *Y Côr Mawr* returned by train to Aberdare they were given the kind of welcome Cup Final winners get today. As Caradog waved the famous Challenge Trophy, the Rifle Corps fired volleys and bells rang out loudly. Excited crowds waved flags and banners. Newspaper reporters praised 'Cambria's Five Hundred' and poets claimed that Wales had conquered London! Thanks to the tonic sol-fa method, Wales had become 'a Sea of Song'.

A postcard of the Crystal Palace

Caradog

The Challenge Trophy

4

Religious Revival

It is March 1905. We have come to a chapel in Neath to see Evan Roberts, one of Wales's most popular revivalist preachers. He is a miner's son who believes that God has been sending him messages. In a vision he saw an outstretched hand holding a piece of paper. On the paper was written 100,000. Evan was certain that this was God's way of telling him to save the souls of 100,000 sinners in Wales. He began to preach in chapels all over Wales. Almost overnight he became a popular hero. People came from far and near to hear him.

From Amlwch in Anglesey to Treorchy in Glamorgan the sounds of religious revival were heard.

The chapel at Neath is bursting at the seams. There are so many people here that we have to stand in the aisle. It is an emotional scene. All around us we hear joyful singing and prayer. As the hymns are sung, Evan Roberts walks up and down the aisle, swinging his arms and clapping his hands. He is a tall, handsome man with sharp, piercing eyes. He is wearing a top coat, a collar and a blue tie. His

A revival service in a coal mine

voice is trembling with emotion as he cries 'Bend us, oh Lord! Bend us!' Men and women are sobbing. We can see tears pouring down their cheeks. Cries of 'Amen' and 'Thanks be to Him' ring out loudly.

As the congregation sings 'Here is love in copious torrents', young women come forward and sink to their knees before Evan Roberts. 'Oh Lord, take me', they cry, as they beg for forgiveness. As they confess their sins, two of Evan Roberts's lady followers – Annie and Maggie Davies – begin to sing sweetly. People clap, wave handkerchiefs, and cry out 'I am a sinner – help me.' One old man beside us leaps to his feet and shouts loudly: 'Nail the flag to the mast, boys.' It's so hot inside the chapel that some of the windows break. Worshippers tell us that they can feel the fire burning in their hearts. It's a stirring experience. As we leave, the congregation is singing 'Have you seen Him?' We are told that the meeting will not end until well past midnight.

The religious revival swept through Wales between 1904 and 1905. No one could remember such large congregations. The *Western Mail* sent a team of reporters to prepare items on the emotional scenes in the revivalist meetings. Miners, quarrymen, farmers, shopkeepers, mothers and children

talked about 'revival' for days. Evan Roberts was treated like a modern pop star. He won thousands of converts and persuaded young people to visit their neighbours and persuade them to come to chapel.

The effect of his preaching tours was remarkable. People flocked to the chapel and prayed and sang with great fervour. Even prize-fighters, drunkards and gamblers were in favour of prayer meetings. Weeping sinners walked through the streets singing hymns loudly. Prayer meetings were held down coal-mines. Young rugby players burnt their jerseys and promised never to play again. When Jenkin Thomas heard Evan Roberts preach at Kenfig Hill, he said: 'I used to play full-back for the Devil, but now I'm forward for God.' Members of the rugby club at Treorchy formed a 'footballers class' in the local Sunday School. Thousands of people claimed that the love of God was filling their souls.

In the autumn of 1905, however, Evan Roberts fell ill. He was a very tired man. The number of revivalist meetings declined and chapel-going lost its appeal. Nowadays many large chapels are nearly empty on Sundays. Some of them have closed down and been converted into garages or cinemas. Only rarely do we hear joyful singing and prayers in Welsh chapels. Some chapel-goers are certain that a religious revival like that of 1904–5 will happen again in Wales. Do you agree? If so, what form do you think it might take?

Many chapels in Wales are now derelict

The Sporting Life

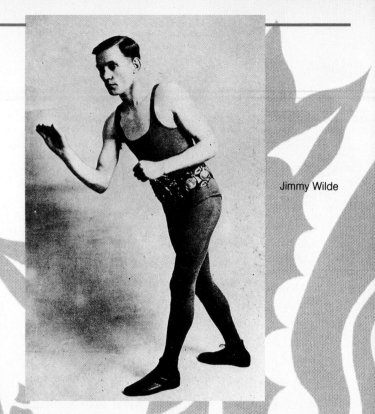

Jimmy Wilde

Life in the industrial valleys of South Wales was not just about eisteddfodau, chapel-going, choral singing and brass bands. Working people also loved sport. They enjoyed pigeon and greyhound racing, playing darts, cross-country running, and prize-fighting. But the most popular sports were rugby, boxing and association football, and in each of these Wales was producing famous stars.

On 16 December, 1905, Wales met New Zealand for the first time on a rugby field. The game was played in the Arms Park in Cardiff. The *Western Mail* said it was 'the most fateful day in the history of rugby in Wales.' The All Blacks were a very successful team and many experts said they were unbeatable. But Wales, too, had tough forwards and skilful runners. In the Welsh fifteen there were colliers, tinplaters and boilermakers. A crowd of 47,000 packed into the Arms Park to support them.

It was a hard, fast game, with players on both sides running swiftly and tackling ferociously. After twenty-five minutes the crowd

went wild with excitement. Dickie Owen, the tiny, stocky Welsh scrum half, broke away to the right, changed direction to the left, and then passed the ball to Cliff Pritchard. The ball was passed on quickly to Rhys Gabe and then to the speedy winger Teddy Morgan. Morgan was twenty yards from the line. Pursued by the All Blacks he ran like a hare and dived over in the corner. What a try! Red Dragon flags were waved in the crowd and hats and leeks were thrown into the air. From then on Wales defended bravely and held out to win 3–0. New Zealand played 32 games on the tour and lost only once – against Wales! Almost overnight Wales became a famous rugby-playing nation.

Boxing, too, was popular because it called for skill, fitness and discipline. Coalminers could earn a few extra pounds by fighting in boxing booths set up in travelling fairs. One of them was Jimmy Wilde, who grew up to be the finest little boxer in the world. Jimmy was born in 1892 at Pont-y-gwaith, near Tylorstown in Glamorgan. Like most of his friends, he became a collier. His great ambition was to become a professional boxer. Dai Davies, an old prizefighter, taught him all the tricks of the boxing ring and Jimmy offered to fight at local boxing

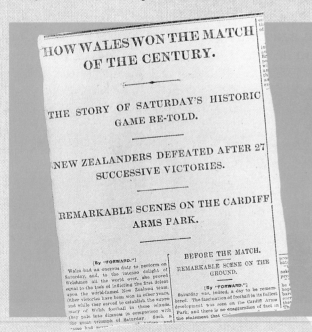

HOW WALES WON THE MATCH OF THE CENTURY.

THE STORY OF SATURDAY'S HISTORIC GAME RE-TOLD.

NEW ZEALANDERS DEFEATED AFTER 27 SUCCESSIVE VICTORIES.

REMARKABLE SCENES ON THE CARDIFF ARMS PARK.

booths. But people laughed when they saw his skinny body. Some said he belonged with the dwarfs in a circus. But Jimmy silenced all his critics by outwitting and outpunching his rivals in the boxing ring. One night, in a boxing booth at Pontypridd fair, he beat 23 opponents, one after another!

Jimmy Wilde was a tiny man – 1.58 metres tall and weighing 48.97 kilos – but he had the heart of a giant. In exhibition bouts he often beat men who were three or four stones heavier. He became known as 'the ghost with the hammer in both hands'. He turned professional in 1913 and a year later he won the flyweight championship of Britain. But his biggest moment came in 1916 when he beat the Zulu Kid in the eleventh round to win the flyweight championship of the world. He remained champion for the next seven years. In his career Jimmy Wilde fought 864 contests – and lost only four times! No wonder the skilful little Welshman was known all over the world as 'the Mighty Atom'.

Association football was also 'the people's game'. By 1910 there were 262 football clubs in South Wales, and in that year Cardiff City began playing at Ninian Park. In 1921 they reached the First Division of the English Football League. But the biggest day in the history of the club was 23 April, 1927. On that day Fred Keenor, the Cardiff captain, led out his team at Wembley on Cup Final day. Cardiff's opponents were the mighty Arsenal. Thousands of Welsh supporters, wearing blue and white rosettes and daffodils, sang the Welsh National Anthem. They sang it so well that King George V asked them to sing it again!

The game was a closely-fought battle. Both defences were on top and there were few goalmouth incidents. But then, out of the blue, Hughie Ferguson of Cardiff shot for goal. It wasn't a very powerful shot but Arsenal's goalkeeper, Dan Lewis (a Welshman from Maerdy!), fumbled the ball. It slipped from his grasp and bounced over the line. It was a lucky goal but it was enough to win the game. For the first and only time, the English Football Association Cup had been won by a club from Wales. Fred Keenor held up the Cup and told reporters: 'This is the biggest day of my life.' As you can guess, the celebrations went on for days in the city of Cardiff!

Fred Keenor with the cup

Hughie Ferguson's goal

The Black Chair

Above: The Black Chair

Left: 'Over the Top', a painting by John Nash of trench warfare in 1917

At the National Eisteddfod held in Birkenhead in September 1917 a huge crowd packed into the pavilion to cheer the chaired poet. Dyfed, the Archdruid, told them that the winner's nickname was 'Fleur-de-lis'. He then called on 'Fleur-de-lis' to stand up when the trumpet sounded. He called three times, but nobody stood. Choking over his words, Dyfed then announced that the winner was a Welsh soldier who had been killed in France. The audience were stunned and many were in tears. The chair was draped in black as people paid tribute to Hedd Wyn, the 'Poet of the Black Chair'.

Hedd Wyn's real name was Ellis Humphrey Evans. He was a shepherd from Trawsfynydd in Merioneth, but his real love was writing poetry. He was a gentle man and everyone liked him. But his life was to change when Britain went to war against Germany in August 1914. Young Welshmen were called

on to enlist in the armed forces. Posters were pinned up telling young men that they now had a chance to become heroes like Prince Llywelyn and Owain Glyndŵr. The war lasted for four years and during that time 272,000 Welshmen joined the armed forces. But some people spoke up against the war and refused to fight. So in May 1916 the government passed a law saying that every fit and able man between 18 and 45 must join the armed forces. Hedd Wyn was one of those who hated war and didn't want to fight. But in January 1917 he was ordered to join the 15th Battalion of the Royal Welsh Fusiliers.

A few months before he was called up, Hedd Wyn began composing a poem called 'The Hero'. But now he was taught how to carry a rifle, use a bayonet, and march properly. His regiment was sent to France to fight the Germans. While he was there, Hedd Wyn used every spare moment to complete his poem. Once it was done he posted it to the organizers of the Birkenhead Eisteddfod. He'd set his heart on winning the chair. But Hedd Wyn never returned to Wales. During the battle for Pilkem Ridge, on 31 July, 1917, he was killed by a mortar shell. He was just thirty years old. A telegram was sent to his parents informing them that 61117, Pte. Ellis Humphrey Evans, RWF, had been killed in action.

Before he died, Hedd Wyn saw great suffering in the muddy trenches of France. Tens of thousands of soldiers were killed or wounded. In his poem 'War', Hedd Wyn wrote:

'And there, the weeping willow trees
Bear the old harps that sang amain,
The lads' wild anguish fills the breeze,
Their blood is mingled with the rain.'

Life on the battlefield was terrible. Soldiers were ordered by their generals to stand in long rows of muddy trenches. They were often up to their knees in mud. It was like fighting in a swamp. Numbed with cold, they had no chance to change their sodden clothes or have a bath. Maggots and lice were a constant nuisance and rats scuttled up and down the trenches. Food had to be kept in tin boxes. From time to time soldiers received chocolate, biscuits, cake, tobacco and cigarette papers from their relatives back home. This made a pleasant change from bully beef and stale bread. At night soldiers whistled and sang to keep their spirits up. On a still night they would shout insults at German soldiers in the trench-es beyond 'no man's land'. Groups of soldiers were also regularly ordered to repair trenches, mend barbed wire, set trip-wires, and carry rations and stores.

The worst part was waiting for the signal to advance. Trembling with cold and fear, soldiers waited in silence for the order to go 'over the top' to challenge the German troops. The suspense was terrible, and you can imagine how Hedd Wyn must have felt. When the signal came, soldiers staggered out of the trenches and made their way forward. They kept their heads down in the face of rapid bursts of rifle fire and machine gun fire. Mortar bombs and bullets whizzed overhead. Poisonous gas drifting through the air made soldiers feel sick and giddy.

Soldiers went like lambs to the slaughter. They were mown down by machine guns, blown to bits by explosive shells, or caught in barbed wire and shot by snipers. Soon the ground was covered with wounded, dying or dead men. Headless and armless men lay silently in puddles of water. Many screamed and moaned in pain. Red Cross men carrying stretchers tended to the wounded and carried away dead bodies. Those who survived to tell the story said it was like hell on earth.

The Great War ended on 11 November, 1918. Since then a remembrance ceremony is held every year on the Sunday which falls closest to that date. Thousands of young men who returned had been badly wounded and scarred. None of them ever forgot the horrors of life in the trenches of France and Belgium. Nor did they forget their brave friends who died in battle. In August 1923 a monument to Hedd Wyn was unveiled in Trawsfynydd. The Welsh poet, R. Williams Parry, sang in memory of the hero who was laid to rest by 'the black trench':

'Grave the bard underground overseas,
    hands
Clasped ever together;
Keen eyes beneath a close lid
Eyes unable to open.'

A stretcher party wades through the mud

4

The Blitz

Welsh soldiers who took part in the Great War of 1914–18 were told that this was a war to end all wars. But it didn't turn out that way. Another ghastly World War began in September 1939 when Britain declared war on Germany. This time we'll find out what life was like for those who stayed at home. A middle-aged man who has lived in Swansea all his life will tell us what he remembers about the war years in the 1940's.

'Times were hard. We were given ration books which said how many ounces of meat, butter, bacon, cheese, sugar, milk, eggs and jam we were supposed to have. I've got a sweet tooth and I missed a lot of my favourite foods. But my father was a butcher and so we had plenty of meat. There was plenty of bread and potatoes as well.

'It's the bombing I remember best. I'd just had my twelfth birthday when Swansea was blitzed in February 1941. I knew that German planes had been bombing cities like London but I never thought that Swansea would be a target. But now I think about it, we'd had a warning in the middle of January. Some of my footballing chums in Bonymaen told me that their school had been destroyed by German bombers. Worse was to come.

'I was fast asleep one night when my father burst into my bedroom to wake me and my brother up. We could hear the warning sirens wailing. We dressed quickly and went down to the Anderson shelter at the bottom of the garden. I remember seeing searchlights lighting up the sky. Dad said we'd be safe in the shelter, but my mother looked very scared. I made sure my cat and dog were safely inside before we shut the door. It was cold and damp in the shelter and we couldn't sleep. We could

hear muffled bangs and explosions. Some of them sounded too close for comfort. I remember praying silently, though I didn't admit to my brother I was scared stiff. Just after two in the morning things quietened down and we fell asleep. When we got up early next morning we had the shock of our lives. Our house was as flat as a pancake. I remember Dad saying "Oh my God, it's all gone!" My mother's first reaction was to say "Oh! I put a new pound of butter on the floor in the kitchen and now it's all been destroyed!" She then burst into tears.

'Many houses had been hit in our street, but no one had been killed. Most of them had spent the night in the public shelter. Dad went off to make sure that all our neighbours were unhurt. When the war first began he'd joined the Local Defence Volunteers. We used to tease him by calling them the "Look, Duck and

An artist's impression of Swansea during the blitz

A photograph of Swansea's wrecked buildings

Vanish'' men, but the volunteers did a lot of good work. Later on they became known as the Home Guard, and Dad enjoyed playing at soldiers by dressing up in his cap, denims and arm-band. He went to special training centres to fight mock battles and to learn to handle firearms and grenades. He spent a lot of time fighting fires and rescuing people. One night a bomb came down in a street in Swansea and set a gas main alight. But Dad jumped on it and smothered the flames. He was good at keeping watch. He had to help the air raid wardens to enforce the black-out regulations. If he saw a glimmer of light in a house he used to hammer on the door and give the occupants a proper ticking off.

'When my father was certain everyone was alright, he took me with him to the town centre. He was worried about his butcher's stall in the market. I've never seen such a sight. Many houses had been flattened. The streets were full of rubble. Fires blazed everywhere and there was a horrible smell of burning gas. Electric cables had been damaged and telephone lines were down. The police had cordoned off the town centre and we weren't allowed in. They told us there was a danger that an unexploded bomb might blow up. We could see from afar that the town's market had been virtually wiped out. Shops, cafes, restaurants and hotels had been badly damaged. Firefighters were still busily dousing the flames.

'When we got home I remember Dad muttering that we'd lost everything. Hundreds of other families were also homeless. Voluntary services brought in mobile canteens and gave us tea, sandwiches and cakes. Tankers brought in water supplies. Luckily we were able to go to stay with my aunt in Manselton. She was a bit of a fusspot but she made us very welcome.

'For years after the Blitz my father told me lots of stories about the bombing of Swansea. He said that one man had a miraculous escape. An oil bomb fell on his house and he fell on top of it. But he got up and ran out before the bomb exploded into flames. His favourite story was the tale of the bomb which landed in a tailor's shop in the middle of the town. It threw a dummy across the road into a chapel entrance where it landed the right way up!'

During the three-day Blitz on Swansea, 230 people were killed, 309 were injured, and over 700 were made homeless. Five days later, James Griffiths, MP, wrote:

'There is something Hitler cannot destroy. It is our love for the old town. And that love will bring us all rallying round. When the vandals are overthrown and peace comes back to our stricken world we shall join its citizens in building a new, and even better, Abertawe.'

In the early 1950's a huge rebuilding programme was started. A new town centre was built. Today Swansea is a busy, thriving modern city.

Swansea rebuilt

5

Industry: the Old and the New

The Quarrymen

A hundred years ago children in school in North Wales learned to write and count on slates dug from Welsh quarries. By 1898 North Wales was producing 489,000 tons of slate a year in huge quarries like Penrhyn (Bethesda), Dinorwig (Llanberis) and Oakeley (Blaenau Ffestiniog). The slates produced were not only used to roof houses. They were needed for making slabs, door steps, laboratory tables and even billiard tables. The Penrhyn Quarry, overlooking the Ogwen Valley, was one of the biggest in the world. 2,800 men worked there in 1900. Here is a good description of their place of work:

An early photograph of the quarry

PENRHYN QUARRY.

BLASTING REGULATIONS.

Blasting shall take place at the above Quarry at the times stated below, viz.

SIGNALS FOR BLASTING.

1. A Bell and Bugle shall be sounded at the commencement of the blasting period, and all persons not engaged in firing shall at once retire to proper shelters.

2. After the lapse of two minutes the Bell and Bugle shall be sounded, and the men engaged in firing shall at once ignite the fuse of their shots and then retire to shelter.

3. After the lapse of four minutes, Bell and Bugle shall be sounded, and this shall mean that all blasting has ceased and that the men should return to work.

E. A. YOUNG.

PORT PENRHYN,
BANGOR.

CHWAREL Y PENRHYN.

RHEOLAU SAETHU.

Cymer Saethu le yn y Chwarel uchod ar yr adegau a nodir isod.

ARWYDDION SAETHU.

1. Bydd i gloch a bugle gael eu swnio ar ddechreu adeg saethu, ac mae pawb na fyddant yn tanio i fyned ar unwaith i le priodol o ddiogelwch.

2. Yn mhen dau funyd bydd i'r gloch a'r bugle gael eu swnio, a bydd i'r rhai fydd yn tanio roddi tân ar fuse eu hergydion, ac yna dianc i ddiogelwch.

3. Yn mhen pedwar munyd swnir y gloch a'r bugle a golyga hyny fod y saethu drosodd, a bod y dynion i ddychwelyd at eu gwaith.

E. A. YOUNG.

PORT PENRHYN,
BANGOR.

'You stand on the brink of an open pit, with irregular sides, jagged with projections of slate rock. Above you and in front rise successive scarpings of the mountain-side. The horizontal lines which, at a distance, appear to stretch like cobwebs at even intervals across the upper workings, are now discovered to be platforms running from end to end. Each forms the base of a separate quarry, along which is a tramway. On these lines horses and trucks are visible. Between these lines, on the vertical face of the rugged rock, men work suspended by ropes slung from the platform below. These are then removed to the wings, where the slate blocks are selected, and the rubble tilted over.'

It sounds like hard and dangerous work! The quarrymen worked at least 50 hours a week in order to earn enough money to make a living.

They worked in groups of four usually.

There were two rockmen, a splitter and a dresser. They were paid by what was called a bargain system. First of all, the four men would sit down to discuss terms with the steward. After arguing for ages they would agree to spend a month working an area of rock, usually about six yards wide, for an agreed wage. A lot depended on the quality of the rock because they were given a bonus for producing lots of slates. Quarrymen who found a good 'bargain' compared it with a Welsh dresser. Just as there were large and small plates on a Welsh dresser, so there were large and small slates on a good bargain.

The rockmen worked on galleries called *ponciau*. Often a gallery would be named after a certain person – perhaps a local character or the daughter of the manager. First of all the rockmen drilled slot-holes into the rock and placed explosive charges in them. This wasn't as easy as it sounds. The explosives had to be measured properly and put in exactly the right place in case they shattered the rock completely. Once this was done a bell or whistle sounded, and the men hurried to the shelter huts. The next thing they heard was the huge roar of the explosion. Four minutes later another bell rang to tell them it was safe to return to the quarry face.

But the danger wasn't over yet. The blast had loosened huge slabs of slate and the rockman now had to prise away the blocks with a crowbar. This was very dangerous because it had to be done whilst hanging from a rope. An example of what could happen next is described in *Y Cychwyn*, a famous novel written by T. Rowland Hughes:

'Robert Ellis laughed and gripped the rope's tail and unhitched it from the pillar.

'One good shove will do the job, George,' he said, as he laid the rope on the rock face.

'Pass me that iron bar after I've got up.'

When he was about ten feet up, small stones began to slide, and Owen thought that the fold was bending.

'Heavens, look out, Bob, look out,' cried George Hobley. Robert Ellis put his foot against the face of the bargain to push himself off. Terrified, he let the rope fall and jumped. He landed on his feet on the hard level of the floor, his head shaking like a doll as he made contact. And then he fell on his back and hit his head cruelly on a jagged piece of rock. He lay terribly still immediately below the fold which was about to fall.'

An engraving showing the gallery system at Penrhyn quarry

When blocks of slate were prised away safely, they were passed on to the splitter. The splitter was a very skilful man. He cut up the blocks, using iron hammers and wedges. Then he split the blocks by tapping them with a chisel and an iron-bound mallet. The splitter had to know how hard to tap in order to split the blocks properly. Then it was the dresser's turn. He cut and trimmed the slates to various sizes with a knife. Most slates were blue, but some of them were green or grey or mottled. They were divided according to their size, and different sizes were called Queens, Princesses, Duchesses, Countesses and Ladies. The finished slates were finally loaded onto wagons and taken to waiting ships. Welsh slates were famous all over the world.

Other workers were also employed in the quarry. The rubblemen were usually older than the others and sometimes in poor health. They didn't have their own bargains and so they relied on the rockmen to give them slabs of rock to convert into slates. Many young boys began work as rubblers and their job was to cart away the waste rock. The quarry also employed men who worked as weighers, hauliers, engine drivers, carpenters, blacksmiths, and storekeepers.

1900.
PENRHYN QUARRIES.
WORKING HOURS.

1900		FROM	TO
January	1st to January	6th, 7 50 a.m.	4 30 p.m.
January	8th to January	13th, 7 50 a.m.	4 40 p.m.
January	15th to January	20th, 7 45 a.m.	4 50 p.m.
January	22nd to January	27th, 7 45 a.m.	5 0 p.m.
January	29th to February	3rd, 7 35 a.m.	5 10 p.m.
February	5th to February	10th, 7 20 a.m.	5 30 p.m.
February	12th to February	17th, 7 10 a.m.	5 30 p.m.
February	19th to October	13th, 7 0 a.m.	5 30 p.m.
October	15th to October	20th, 7 0 a.m.	5 20 p.m.
October	22nd to October	27th, 7 0 a.m.	5 10 p.m.
October	29th to November	3rd, 7 10 a.m.	5 0 p.m.
November	5th to November	10th, 7 20 a.m.	4 45 p.m.
November	12th to November	17th, 7 25 a.m.	4 30 p.m.
November	19th to November	24th, 7 30 a.m.	4 25 p.m.
November	26th to December	1st, 7 35 a.m.	4 20 p.m.
December	3rd to December	8th, 7 40 a.m.	4 20 p.m.
December	10th to December	15th, 7 50 a.m.	4 20 p.m.
December	17th to December	22nd, 7 50 a.m.	4 20 p.m.
December	24th to December	29th, 7 50 a.m.	4 20 p.m.

NO WORK AFTER NOON ON SATURDAYS.

MEAL HOUR **12** NOON TO **1** P.M.
(BOYS UNDER 18, 11 TO 12 O'CLOCK.)

Blasting Hours.
ON AND AFTER MONDAY, JANUARY 1st, 1900.
9 a.m., 11 a.m., 12 noon, 12.55 p.m., 3.0 p.m.
When the BELL for ceasing work sounds at 5.0 p.m. or later, blasting is allowed at 4.0 p.m. (*vide Rules for Blasting Operations*)

PAY DAYS DURING THE YEAR 1900.

January	27th	August	11th
February	24th	September	8th
March	24th	October	6th
April	21st	November	3rd
May	19th	December	1st
June	16th	December	29th
July	14th		

HOLIDAYS.

Good Friday	April 13th	Whit-Monday	June 4th
Saturday	April 14th	Harvest Thanksgiving	
Easter Monday	April 16th	Christmas Day	Dec. 25th
Ascension-day	May 24th		

PENRHYN QUARRIES,
December 1st, 1899.
E. A. YOUNG.

An early engraving of the quarry

Welsh quarrymen were very proud of their skills in gauging rock and using a chisel and mallet. One popular song went like this:

‘You must have Welshmen
    to break the stone
For the rock doesn’t understand English.’

In Gwynedd in 1891 nearly 7 of every 10 persons over the age of two spoke *only* Welsh. Welsh was the language of the quarry, the home, the street, the chapel and the playground. During their lunch-time break many quarrymen met in the *caban*, a kind of canteen where they ate their food and drank tea. One of them claimed that the men drank ‘tea for breakfast, tea for lunch, tea for tea, and tea for supper’. Their meals were very meagre. A quarryman and his family usually ate potatoes, eggs, bread and butter and perhaps a little cheese and bacon. Meat was eaten only on Sundays. They had very few fresh vegetables. It’s no wonder, therefore, that so many quarrymen fell ill. They suffered from malnutrition and stomach pains. At work, too, they inhaled so much dust that they often found it difficult to breathe.

The *caban* wasn’t just a canteen. It was also a concert hall, a theatre and an eisteddfod pavilion! Over lunch the quarrymen entertained one another by singing hymns, folk-songs and *cerdd dant*, reciting poetry and passages from the Bible, and miming and acting. General knowledge quizzes and spelling competitions were very popular, and there were always loud arguments about religion and politics. Many quarrymen regularly went to Sunday Schools and listened to sermons in chapel. During the week they went to society meetings and the Band of Hope. There were 22 chapels within three miles of the centre of Bethesda. But there were also more than 40 pubs, and the quarryman covered in dust liked to quench his thirst with a pint of beer.

The quarrymen were very independent people who liked to stand up for their rights. They came together in 1874 to set up the North Wales Quarrymen’s Union. At that time Lord Penrhyn, the wealthy owner of the Penrhyn Quarry, treated his workers quite fairly. The men respected him and called him ‘yr Hen Lord’ – ‘the Old Lord’. But before he died in 1885 Lord Penrhyn warned the quarrymen to beware of his son, George Sholto Douglas Pennant, who was to succeed him as the second Lord Penrhyn.

He said: ‘Beware that you do not offend George, for if you do he will never forgive; he can never forgive.’ His words were soon to come true.

Loading slate on to a ship in 1896

5

The Great Strike 1900–1903

NOTICE.

Inasmuch as a number of the Penrhy
Quarry Employees has during the last for
night actively participated in certain acts
violence and intimidation against some
their fellow-workmen and officials, and to-da
nearly all the Employees have left their wor
without leave, Notice is hereby given tha
such Employees are suspended for 14 days.

E. A. YOUNG

PORT PENRHYN,
Bangor, November 6th, 1900.

Chwarel y Penrhyn.

RHYBUDD.

nt ag i nifer o weithwyr Chwarel
n ystod y pythefnos diweddaf
weithredol mewn ymosodiadau
bygythiadau yn erbyn rhai o'u
a swyddogion, ac heddyw i agos
eithwyr adael eu gwaith heb
ldir Rhybudd drwy hyn fod y
wyr yn cael eu hatal am bedwar-
eg.

E. A. YOUNG

YN,
chwedd 6ed, 1900.

The second Lord Penrhyn was a very rich man. He lived in a huge castle a mile outside Bangor. His estate consisted of 72,000 acres. He spoke no Welsh at all, and the manager of the Penrhyn Quarry, E. A. Young, was also an Englishman. Lord Penrhyn was a powerful and stubborn man who didn't like trade unions. The quarrymen didn't like him or trust him. They often complained to him about the bargain system. Some men were earning more than others, especially if they were ready to bribe the quarry officials. But Lord Penrhyn refused to listen to the quarrymen's complaints. As long as his profits amounted to thousands of pounds, he was more than content.

Things got worse in October 1900 when Lord Penrhyn sacked 26 quarrymen after a dispute about contracts. The men were charged and brought before magistrates in Bangor on 5 November. Hundreds of quarrymen marched into the centre of the town to support them. Outside the courts they sang their favourite hymn, 'Oh Lord God, Providence'. Lord Penrhyn was furious and he punished his workers by locking them out of the quarry for fourteen days. The quarrel continued and, on 22 November, 2,800 quarrymen decided to come out on strike. The strike was to last for three years. It was known as *Streic Fawr Bethesda* (The Great Strike of Bethesda).

The quarrymen went to see Lord Penrhyn to tell him their demands. They wanted the right to discuss their grievances properly, like other trade unions. They urged him to re-employ sacked quarrymen, give them decent wages, and treat them as men. But Lord Penrhyn was as stubborn as a mule. He said

Top: Notice of suspension
Above: Lord Penrhyn
Right: The union badge

that he expected all his workers to be loyal and obedient to him. He refused to budge an inch, and so the strike went on and on. The quarrymen were determined to win. One of them said:

'A man must be respected as a man and as a worker by every squire and lord in this country.'

Quarry officials, helped by clergymen, tried to persuade the quarrymen to return to work. Some families were close to starvation and so some workers broke the strike. By June 1901, around 550 quarrymen had gone back to work. On 11 June, Lord Penrhyn rode on horseback to the quarry and gave each worker a gold sovereign. Those who were still on strike called it 'The Traitor's Pound', and they sang this song to the tune *Y Mochyn Du*:

'Heard you then the dreadful story
Dire treason and conspiracy,
Worse far worse than any other
Is the effect of blackleg bother.
   Chorus
As we watch with heavy heart!
As we watch with heavy heart!
For a single golden sovereign
Blacklegs sell themselves at mart.'

Those who had gone back to work were booed and jostled by striking quarrymen. Their names were printed in local newspapers and they were turned away by shopkeepers and told not to come to chapel. They were called *cynffonwyr* (blacklegs) and *bradwyr* (traitors). Quarrymen on strike placed cards in the windows of their homes:

THERE IS
NO TRAITOR
IN THIS HOUSE

From time to time there were angry scuffles and fights, and constables and soldiers were needed to keep order.

Most of the quarrymen stayed out on strike. W. J. Parry, one of their supporters, called on them to stand firm:

'We must not lower our banner now. It must be a fight to the death with this tyrant. He will stoop to anything to gain his end. He gave each of the men who returned to work during the lock-out a golden sovereign. Who but Lord Penrhyn would have done this? His friends say that he is a good sportsman, but evidently he can strike below the belt.'

Lord Penrhyn was so angry when he read Parry's words that he took him to court and was awarded £500. But Parry and others carried on fighting. An appeal for money was launched and thousands of pounds were collected to help poor families. Three large choirs from Bethesda travelled all over Britain to raise money at concerts. They raised over £32,000.

Fellow workers in other industries, especially in South Wales, sent large sums of money to help the quarrymen.

But as time went on families found it impossible to live. There wasn't enough money to buy food, clothes and fuel. Many quarrymen went to look for work in the coal mines of South Wales. Others emigrated to America. In the end the quarrymen were defeated by hunger. Slowly they began to trickle back to work. On 14 November, 1903, the struggle ended. People in Bethesda were very angry and disappointed that the quarrymen had lost. They blamed the blacklegs for betraying the strikers. There are still some people who call 11 June 'the traitors' birthday'.

Lord Penrhyn refused to let all the strikers return to work. By 1907 only 1,800 men were employed at the Penrhyn Quarry, and after 1918 the slate industry began to decline.

Foreign markets were lost, and tiles made of cement and asbestos became more popular. Not until the 1980's did demand for slate from the Penrhyn Quarry begin to grow once more. In 1988, around 24,000 tons of slate were produced. Can you work out how much more was produced in the whole of North Wales in 1898?

John Hughes of Yuzovka

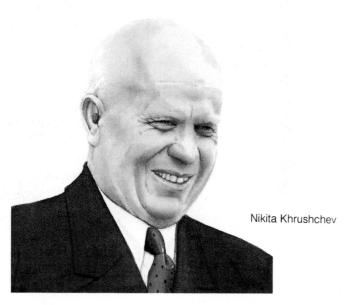

Nikita Khrushchev

In 1894 a boy called Nikita Khrushchev was born in a mud hut in Russia. He was a miner's son. Many years later, between 1958 and 1964, he was the premier of the USSR.In his life-story he remembered the days when his father worked in the coal mines in a town called Yuzovka:

'I knew from my childhood that the British were first class steelmen. Yuzovka, the town where I grew up, was named after the owner of the local steel factory – the Welshman Hughes!'

Who was this Welshman called Hughes? His full name was John Hughes and he used to work for the Crawshay family before he became manager of an engineering works in Newport. His company was well-known for making ships' anchors and chains. He then moved to London to become general manager of an engineering and shipbuilding company at Millwall Docks. His speciality there was making tough armourplate for British battleships.

The iron shields which John Hughes produced were so good that the Russian govern-ment invited him to help them. Russia didn't have any railways and her industries were small and poor. Most iron and steel in Russia was shipped there from South Wales and this was proving very expensive. So, in April 1869, John Hughes formed the New Russia Company. Its aim was to produce more iron and coal, and to develop railways in Russia.

John Hughes had decided that the best place to settle was the Donetz Basin in the Ukraine. There was plenty of good coal and iron ore there. He made his home in a farm on the banks of the river Kalmius. He also leased land on the other side of the river. He built a smithy and began planning how to build an iron works. Skilled iron workers from South Wales came out to help him in April 1870. Six years later the New Russia Company's ironworks was the largest in Russia, producing 16,000 tons of iron rails a year. Nearly 2,000 people worked in what was now called 'Hughes's Factory'.

The Russian people who worked for John Hughes were not treated very well. Hughes was a hard master and he made sure that all his workers obeyed his orders. Men, women and children worked for up to sixteen hours a day. Most of the poorly paid labourers lived in damp, filthy, and overcrowded dug-outs. They were described like this:

The city of Donetsk

Labourers in Hughes's works

'The walls were of stone without plaster of any kind, the roof was made of reeds and the floor was bare earth. Single men slept on common plank beds, perhaps fifty or sixty of them in tiers. Workers with families were given one room, no matter how many children they had, and there was a common kitchen with a fire place and coal stove for six families.'

You can't blame the Russian workers for calling these houses 'The Kennels' (*Sobachevka*). There was no clean water or sewerage of any kind. Many families became ill and children died of cholera, dysentery and typhoid.

But John Hughes's industries went from strength to strength. The town which grew up around his works was called Yuzovka (or Hughesovka). Over 48,000 people lived there by 1910.

When John Hughes died, aged 74, in 1889, his four sons took over the management of the works. After the Russian Revolution in 1917 the Soviet government took over John Hughes's companies. In 1924 they changed Yuzovka's name to Stalino. Then, in 1961, they changed it from Stalino to Donetsk.

Today, Donetsk is a modern coal-mining town with its own medical school, university, theatres, shops and restaurants. Perhaps some of its people, like Nikita Khrushchev, remember that their town was first built by a Welshman. John Hughes used to say that the Welsh people were stick-in-the-muds. 'They stick at home and never learn anything of the great world outside.' In Hughes's day, people who decided to leave Wales usually went to America. But John Hughes was brave enough to venture to the east and help the Russian people to build new industries.

Wales Yesterday and Today

Bessemer steel-making in the 1870's

Making steel today

The East Moors steelworks

Angharad's class is doing a history project. The children have been told to find out how life has changed over the last fifty years.

'You could start by talking to your grandparents,' suggests Mrs. Kyffin, Angharad's teacher.

In the evening Angharad and her mum go to visit Grandfather. He lives in an old part of Cardiff called Splott.

'So you want to know what life was like when I was young?' laughs Grandfather. 'You'd better come in and see what I can remember.' Soon they are sitting in front of a bright coal fire. Grandfather thinks hard before beginning his story. 'I was born in 1921. My mother and father – your great-grandparents – lived in Dowlais near Merthyr. My dad worked in the steelworks.'

'Did your mum have a job, too?' asks Angharad.

'You must be joking! I was the youngest of nine brothers and sisters. Mum spent every minute of the day washing, cleaning, baking, ironing, mending clothes, and trying to make ends meet. It was certainly a tough life for the women in those days. But then it was for everyone. Remember, in the 1920's nobody had washing machines, electric kettles, vacuum cleaners, fridges – all the things you have at home. Everything had to be done by hand, and took much, much longer.'

'When did you come to live in Splott?'

'I've always lived here. My parents moved to Splott the year before I was born. Dad had heard about the new steelworks here in Cardiff and he and my older brothers wanted to try for jobs here. Dad was worried about Dowlais because the iron ore in that area was almost used up. Cardiff was a good place to build a new steelworks. Iron ore could be brought from other countries and unloaded at the docks nearby. Dowlais is twenty miles inland. It would have been too expensive to carry the iron ore all that way. It was a good job my family did move. In 1930 the Dowlais works closed down, and over three thousand men and women lost their jobs. It was terrible.'

'What was your school like?' asks Angharad.

'Well, at your school all the lessons are taught in Welsh. At my school they were all in English. There were no Welsh schools in those days. My parents spoke Welsh to each other – especially when they didn't want me to know what they were saying – but they never spoke Welsh to me. Everybody thought that it was only English-speakers who got on in life. But I left school when I was fourteen and went as an apprentice to the East Moors steelworks. Most of my life I worked on the converter.'

'What's a converter, Grandad?'

'Well, it's a big furnace. It looks a bit like a giant concrete pear. It turns molten iron into steel. My job was to pour the white-hot steel from the converter into huge moulds. The steel cools and sets into the blocks we call ingots. The work was very dangerous and the heat was almost unbearable. We used to sweat buckets! So we needed to drink a great deal and take salt tablets every day. That's why I still

like my beer, I suppose. I used to start work at ten o'clock at night and finish at six in the morning. You see, the furnaces were never allowed to go out – except for repairs or cleaning – so as one team of men finished another group started.'

'It must have been very odd going to bed when everybody else was getting up.'

'I got used to it. It was nice to have the afternoons free to work in the garden or the house. I used to have a large allotment as well and this used to keep us well supplied with vegetables. Remember there were no deep freezers, so we shared what we couldn't eat or preserve with the neighbours.'

'How long did you work at East Moors?'

'I had to retire in 1981 when I was sixty. A few years later East Moors was closed down. The Government said that the old works was too old and inefficient to compete with the modern steelworks at Port Talbot and Llanwern. Ebbw Vale and Shotton closed at about the same time. There was nothing anybody could do. The site of the old steelworks has been bulldozed flat. I feel sad each time I see what they have done, but I'm glad that new factories and industries have been built there. They say they are going to build new offices, hotels, and even a marina for yachts in the old Cardiff docks area. There seem to be new buildings everywhere in Cardiff, and I can't believe how the price of houses has gone up. I don't know how you will be able to manage when you grow older.'

Angharad feels a little sad.

'Don't worry,' says Angharad's mum. 'Things don't get better without change.'

The modern factory on the East Moors site

Wales Today and Tomorrow

National Panasonic in Cardiff

Angharad is still working on her history project. She has found out about her grandfather's work. Now she has to find out what sort of work her parents do. Both of them have full-time jobs. Mum works in a factory and Dad works for the Welsh Development Agency.

'What's your job like, Mum?' asks Angharad.

'I work in a new factory that puts television sets together,' says her mother. 'All the parts of the televisions are made in other countries and sent to Wales to be assembled. Most of the workers are women who live in the old coal-mining areas north of Cardiff. They come in to work on the company bus. Some of them have to travel forty miles. There are very few jobs in the valleys, especially for the men who used to work in the mines.'

'Is the work you do fun?'

'Oh no! Not fun exactly,' laughs Mum. 'It's really rather boring. But the wages are better than those paid in most other firms, and we are well looked after by the Japanese company that owns the factory. We get good holidays, good meals, and the factory itself is bright and clean.'

The new Brother factory in Wrexham

'What about your work, Dad?'

'Well, the WDA was set up by the Government to help solve one of the country's most serious problems. Most of the heavy industries in Wales, like steel-making and coal-mining, employ only a fraction of the workers they used to need. There are fewer than six thousand miners left in South Wales today. At one time there were over a quarter of a million. The WDA has to try and replace these old industries with new ones.'

'Why?'

'People need jobs, of course. We have a strong workforce in Wales. If we can't find work for them to do they'll be forced to leave the country to look for jobs. We have to change people's ideas. Our slogan is "High Technology is at home in Wales", but most foreign people still think of South Wales as a dreary place covered with slag heaps. They don't believe it when we tell them about all the new things that are happening here.'

'What are these things?' asks Angharad.

'We now have good roads in South Wales,'

says Mum. 'It's much easier to send the things we make here – like my televisions – all over the world.'

'Exactly!' says Dad. 'The roads in North Wales are also being improved, and this will bring in businesses from all over the world.'

'Won't that mean that everybody will want to speak only English?' asks Angharad. 'Not many foreign people can speak Welsh.'

'I don't think so,' says Mum. 'You go to a Welsh school. More and more people want to speak Welsh. Dad and I had to go to evening classes to learn the Welsh language, but you were brought up as a Welsh-speaker. It's easier now we have the Welsh Television Channel, S4C, and local radio stations and newspapers in Welsh.'

'Remember,' says Dad, 'that Wales has the most beautiful scenery in the British Isles. People want to come here for holidays from all over the world. There are more hotels and places to stay than ever before. And there are more and more places to visit. Visitors want to see castles, fine houses, historic sites and buildings, and we certainly have some of the best in Britain!'

'We mustn't get carried away!' laughs Mum. 'There are still many problems that will have to be solved. Too many people are still out of work. Young people in country areas can't afford to buy houses. Many farms and cottages are bought as second homes by wealthy people and stand empty for most of the year. Because Wales is so beautiful too many people want to retire here. This means that local authorities have to spend money they can't really afford looking after them. Families with young children are moving in from England, and teachers don't find it easy to teach them to speak Welsh. Yes, Wales is changing. It will be up to you and your friends – when you grow up – to see that it keeps changing for the better.'

Nursery school children march in support of the Welsh language

The Inmos factory near Newport

Index